Shape Detection in Computer Vision Using the Hough Transform

Shape Detection in Computer Vision Using the Hough Transform

V.F. LEAVERS

Springer-Verlag
London Berlin Heidelberg New York
Paris Tokyo Hong Kong
Barcelona Budapest

V.F. Leavers, BSc, PhD
Department of Physics
King's College London
The Strand
London WC2R 2LS, UK

TA
1632
L42
1992

ISBN 3–540–19723–0 Springer-Verlag Berlin Heidelberg New York
ISBN 0–387–19723–0 Springer-Verlag New York Berlin Heidelberg

British Library Cataloguing in Publication Data
Leavers, V. F.
Shape Detection in Computer Vision Using the Hough Transform
I. Title
006.3
ISBN 3–540–19723–0

Library of Congress Data available

Typesetting: Camera ready by author
34/3830-543210 (printed on acid-free paper)

PREFACE

Repeated visual inspection tasks, whether industrial or academic, are often tedious and labour intensive but nevertheless require specialist skill and careful judgement. There have been many attempts to automate such processes. However, few have yet made the transition from research topic to production method. One reason for this is that scientists seem to be infatuated with anything mathematical. If something can be expressed as an equation we treat it with profound respect, if it is merely descriptive we tend to be dismissive. Pure research in computer recognition tasks often pursues theories of shape representation and detection as goals in themselves without any concern being given to their computability or to any application specific adaptations. In addition, the availability and applicability of the results of such research is often hampered by the computer vision community failing to recognize that the potential user may lack some of the basic skills needed in either computing or mathematics. This book is aimed in particular at two groups of potential users and the problems they may encounter.

The first group consists of 'non-mathematical' academics who simply want to use computer vision as a tool in their own research programs. Such people may be, for example, cytologists or biologists whose only need for anything mathematical is a good knowledge of statistics. The opportunity to relay useful work to these people can be lost if the computer vision community does not adopt a more enlightened perspective on the comprehensibility of what it is producing. In particular, those of us who routinely use mathematics in our work lose sight of the fact that it is a skill which has to be developed. Some of the more advanced concepts are anything but intuitively obvious, it is only by using them that we are able to understand and manipulate them. Large sections of the book set out to develop the necessary mathematical skills with unashamedly simple, wholly pictorial explanations. These are aimed at developing a strong intuitive understanding of the underlying mathematics before introducing any complicated notation. Anyone who does not need these sections can simply skip them.

The second group are those people in industry. It is often difficult for such people to make use of current research because they lack the background information needed. This makes it difficult to distinguish between genuine trends and commercially inconsequential developments in an area of research. For this reason companies are often reluctant to take on board new advances. Moreover, smaller companies may have to operate within cost constraints which may well be the final arbiters in any decision to implement new technology. If the vision community is to court the patronage of these people we need to respect their situation and be realistic concerning it. With this in mind, the book contains a review of the Hough Transform technique for shape detection. Care is taken to distinguish between research that aims to further basic understanding of the technique without necessarily being computationally realistic and research that may be applicable in an industrial context. Whilst academically, the former may undoubtedly improve the performance of the technique, it often adds significant computational burdens to the overall processing load and this may not be acceptable in industrial or commercial situations.

Both groups of people may need to acquire some feel for the technique. The book ends by recognising this need. A case study is presented in some detail. This shows the new user how to begin an implementation by following a particular algorithm step by step. It includes the prefiltering of the image and the use of edge detectors. More importantly, the case study also shows what can go wrong and how to deal with it. This can save much time and frustration.

This book aims to fill a gap by making available state-of-the-art computer vision techniques using the Hough Transform method of shape detection and recognition. If offers the non-specialist easily assimilated theory plus advice about implementing the technique. It will also be useful to post-graduate students who need an informal but thorough grounding in this area of research.

ACKNOWLEDGEMENTS

I would like to express my gratitude to Professor R.E. Burge, Head of the Physics Department at King's College London, for allowing me use of the departmental facilities. I also thank Dr. Helen Berenyi who proof read the final text. Most of all I would like to thank Nigel Arnot, our departmental systems manager, for all the invaluable help, support and encouragement he has given me.

The text for this book was prepared on equipment provided by a Science and Engineering Research Council Grant (SERC GR/F 92343), 'A buyer's guide to the Hough Transform'. It was typeset using Donald Knuth's TeX.

CONTENTS

LIST OF FIGURES

Appendix 1

Appendix 2

Appendix 4

CHAPTER 1

Computer Vision: Shape Detection

1.1 Why Computer Vision?

The answer to this question is that automation can never achieve its full potential without the aid of artificial sensory perception and of the five senses, vision is perhaps the most important. Repeated visual inspection tasks whether industrial or academic, are often tedious and labour intensive but nonetheless require specialist skill and careful judgement. It is not difficult to see that the automation of such tasks would bring great benefits. Advances in computer technology, sensing devices, image processing and pattern recognition have resulted, in recent years, in better and cheaper visual inspection equipment and automated visual inspection for a wide variety of applications is now in use. If we take a look at just a few of them it will give us an idea of the potential offered by this particular branch of research.

1.1.1 Industrial applications

One of the most difficult, time consuming and labour intensive aspects of mass-production manufacturing is the process of visual inspection. Most automated visual inspection tasks involve repeatedly observing a particular type of object to detect defects. Such examinations seek to identify both functional and cosmetic defects. The automation of visual inspection tasks can therefore increase productivity and improve product quality.

The electronics industry is perhaps the most active in applying automated visual inspection to such products as printed circuit boards (PCBs). Here the boards are inspected to isolate such defects as shorts, opens, over-etching, under-etching and spurious metals. A simple thresholding scheme is used to reduce the PCB grey-level image to a binary image. PCB inspection algorithms fall into two categories, reference-comparison, see for example [Thissen 1977], and design-rule verification [Davidsson et al 1979]. The reference-comparison is a simple template matching technique. The method works well but it is essential that the sample under inspection be precisely aligned. In the design-rule verification it is the dimensions of the various components that are checked. No precise alignment is required but large flaws and distorted features may be missed.

Radiographic analysis, [Wagner 1987], is a commonly used method for the inspection of industrial parts with internal structures. In general, the X-ray images are not high-contrast but exhibit subtle shades of grey thus sophisticated image processing is needed to deal with edge enhancement and noise correction. The design of inspection algorithms is usually tailored to specific applications.

The automatic visual inspection of food products, see [Davies 1990], is another well developed application of machine vision techniques. For example, biscuits may be checked for breakages or in the case of chocolate coated biscuits, a simple check on the dimensions of the biscuit can be used to regulate the thickness of the chocolate coating.

1.1.2 Medical applications

The routine inspection of medical images for the purpose of diagnosis is a tedious and time consuming activity, it nonetheless requires great skill and experience to arrive at correct judgements. The Artificial Intelligence community are constantly improving means by which this expertise may be transferred from the highly skilled individuals concerned to expert systems which may then be used to automate the visual inspection of medical images. Such methods are already emerging as viable aids to treatment.

Clinicians concerned with the treatment of patient's who have abnormalities of the jaw and teeth will first take a standard X-ray of the patients head and then look for particular anatomical features in that X-ray. Knowledge of the type of feature under detection is used to enhance and identify those features. Once they are located, important distances and angles are then automatically measured and the data used to calculate a course of treatment.

Another medical application of machine vision is in the non-destructive evaluation of plastic surgical techniques prior to the trauma of surgery. A laser beam scan is made of the patients head and the data so obtained are used to construct a three-dimensional representation of the patient's head which can then be stored in the computer. This stored representation may then be manipulated to evaluate the results of proposed surgery. Post-operative changes in the distribution of soft tissue can also be quantified using such a technique.

The automated inspection and manipulation of medical images is perhaps one of the most creative and socially acceptable applications of computer vision techniques.

1.1.3 Social applications

The social applications of machine vision are many and diverse. They range from text-to-speech-synthesis for visually impaired people to automatic finger print identification by the police. The automatic recognition of faces for the purposes of security checks is a very active area of current research where the fundamental problems remain largely unresolved.

Perhaps one of the most socially significant applications is in the area of man-machine interfacing via the use of such aids as electronic paper. While this is not machine vision as such, it employs the same techniques used in optical character recognition to translate text, handwritten using a special light pen on a purpose built electronically sensitive surface, into typed text which may then be edited and manipulated with the aid of the special light pen. It is important because it provides a much more natural interface to the computer for people who would normally find it tedious and time consuming to use the conventional keyboard techniques to produce text of a high quality.

1.1.4 Military applications

qindexcomputer vision military applications The military applications of automatic vision systems are many. They include automatic surveillance of enemy territory using data remotely collected by satellite or radar images taken by planes. Autonomous vehicles which may be used in areas unfit for human beings are another aspect of current military research into machine vision.

1.2 Why This Book?

We can see that the applications of machine vision techniques are many and varied. Few however have yet made the transition from the research to the routine laboratory. One reason for this is that pure research in computer vision often pursues theories as goals in themselves without any concern being given to their computability nor to any application specific adaptations. A second reason exists in that much of the effort needed to implement recognition systems is interdisciplinary. If we take a look at the writing on the wall of computer vision, Fig. 1.1 , it would look something like this.

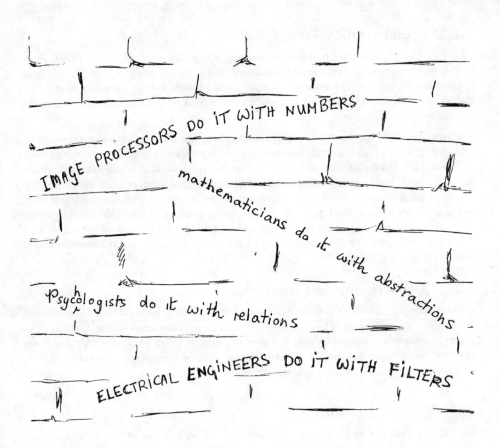

Fig 1.1 *Writing on the Wall of Computer Vision*

Image processors do it with numbers...
They like numerical methods and statistics and probabilities...

Mathematicians do it with abstractions...
They like reducing the world to systems of equations...

Psychologists do it with relations...
They like suggesting relational data structures and the like...

Electrical engineers do it with filters...
Median filters, Hamming filters, any filters...

The potential end user may often be confounded by a screen of professional jargon. In addition, the availability and applicability of the results of research may be hampered by a lack, on the part of the end user, of basic skills in either computing or mathematics. This book is intended to fill partially this gap by making available state of the art computer vision techniques with respect to a particular method of shape detection and recognition, that of the Hough Transform . It will hopefully provide an interface between the expertise needed to initiate low level computer vision tasks associated with the technique and its specialist applications.

1.3 Why the Hough Transform?

Looking at Fig. 1.2 we intuitively know that there is some kind of written message there, if only it could be focused. Fig. 1.3 illustrates that even twenty-twenty vision is still perfectly useless if the viewer does not understand what he is looking at. The need is not simply to *see* but somehow to *decode* the message. In the same way it is clear that vision alone (however perfect) cannot deliver computationally realistic descriptions of a scene, the image must first be processed in order to extract information with which to build symbolic representations of the sort a computer can manipulate. But how exactly do we begin to represent an object symbolically? Object recognition is usually performed using the property of shape as a discriminator. This is where the Hough Transform comes in. It is one way of executing the transition from a visual-stimulus orientated representation (the raw image data) to the symbolic representation of shape necessary for object recognition. It is one method among many. What follows is an illustrated overview of qindexshape detection methods qindexshape detection symbolic representations Shape Detection methods. It places the Hough Transform in context with respect to other shape detection methods and helps us to determine the criteria we might expect to associate with a good representation of shape.

1.4 Representing Shape Symbolically

This section deals with the problem of symbolically representing shape. Theories concerning shape detection are reviewed. The review is by no means exhaustive but rather it is intended to give a moderately detailed, illustrative overview of existing

5

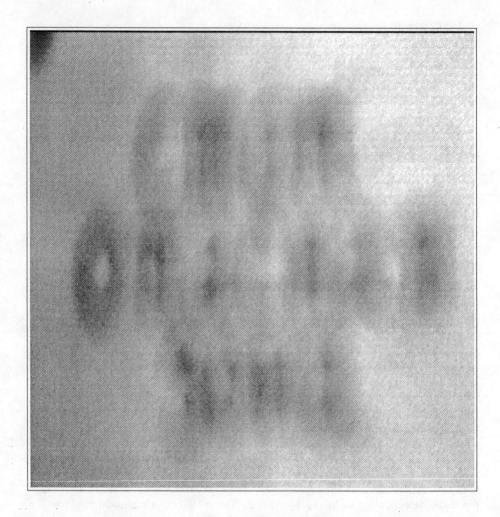

Fig 1.2 *Faulty vision*

Fig 1.3 *Clear vision*

theories and aims to place the Hough Transform in context. From previous solutions to the problems of shape detection certain criteria emerge as being essential to a good representation of shape. A list is compiled from various sources, most notably Marr [Marr 1980], Brady [Brady 1983] and Biedermann [Biedermann 1985]. Items on the list are illustrated by analogy to various writing systems.

There are many methods which claim to extract information about shape from image data. How can we judge them? What properties are we looking for? Human beings are able to transmit and receive symbolic information apparently effortlessly and on the whole very efficiently. We do this in a number of ways. One of the most widely used and understood symbolic representation is that of the written word. We are all familiar with an alphabet of some sort so maybe we should start here. What can we learn from alphabets ? Are there any analogies we can draw to help us in our quest to represent shape symbolically?

To begin with, there are lots of alphabets...
Some are mediocre...
And some are terrible...

直線パターン検出のための Hough 曲線追跡型 アルゴリズムについて

Fig 1.4 *Japanese*

Let's look at a worst case and see why it's a worst case. Without wishing to offend anyone, such a case might be Japanese. It has 10,000 characters. These constitute the primitives of the representation, that is they are its irreducible components. As an alphabet it is almost completely inefficient. Each symbol represents a concept and cannot be decomposed into sub units. The representation is not even portable, that is it cannot cope with abstract concepts from other languages or cultures. We see in the example, Fig. 1.4 , there is no Japanese way of saying **Hough**.

In vision it is the equivalent to **template matching** . This is the most low-level possibility for representing shape. Using this method, a template or reference two-dimensional array is stored which is then matched on a one-to-one basis with the image. This kind of representation is as inefficient as the Japanese alphabet and for the same reason, there is no power to decompose explicit in the representation. So we meet the first criterion in our quest for a good representation of shape.

1.) Decomposition
The power of any representation derives from an allowance of free combinations of components. A set of primitives or irreducible components should therefore be associated with the representation. Where the set of primitives is small, particularly fine discriminations need not be made in the detection process [Biedermann 1985].

An additional disadvantage exists concerning template matching. Each object requires templates that represent all possible locations and orientations of that object within the image space. For example the search for a straight line in image space would involve convolving the image with the templates of all possible straight lines that might exist in the image. This would be very time consuming. To expand the process to include all possible sizes, locations and orientations of shapes would be a formidable computing task and very costly in terms of computer memory. It is clear that in image space, it is not possible to have a unique representation of the general *notion* of a shape only templates of particular shapes in particular orientations and sizes. However, it is a generally accepted principle in computer vision that the symbolic description of an object will be represented in an object centred co-ordinate system but that the image input will be represented in a viewer centred co-ordinate system. Therefore, to be useful, a representation of shape should offer invariance under the operations of translation, rotation and scaling and should make explicit the viewer-object correspondence . We meet our second criterion for a good representation of shape:

2.) Invariance
Information that is the basis of recognition should be invariant to the operations of translation, rotation and scaling.

Another drawback of template matching is that, where many objects are to be detected, large amounts of computer memory are required and the time taken to achieve a match is not commensurate with real-time applications. It is a useful technique only when the images under detection are simple and the objects are uniformly aligned. We now have a third necessary condition.

3.) Accessibility
It is necessary to demonstrate that any proposed representation of shape is computationally realistic [Marr 1980].

A natural progression from the idea of template matching is to that of spatial matched filtering [Rosie 1966]. Mathematically the use of a matched filter corresponds to correlating the image with a function whose form matches that of the object under detection. Davies [Davies 1990] discusses the use of spatial matched filters with respect to object detection in computer vision. It is known [Turin 1960] that when a filter is matched to a given signal, it detects that signal with optimum signal-to-noise ratio under white noise conditions. However, such a noise condition is rarely present in the case of real images. In addition, changes in the background illumination cause significant changes in the signal both from one image to another and from one part of an image to another. The method suffers from the disadvantages associated with template matching in that each new object requires a unique filter and no explicit information concerning shape is made available by this method.

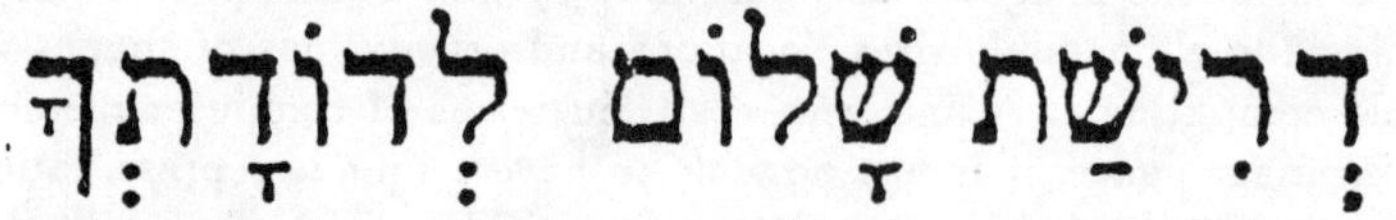

דְּרִישַׁת שָׁלוֹם לְדוֹדָתֵךְ

Fig 1.5 *Hebrew*

What we need is a computationally realistic representation that is invariant to rotation, translation and scaling. In addition we need to be able to decompose our objects into more basic units or primitives. But how should we choose the primitives? How many of them should there be? Let's go back to our analogy and look at another kind alphabet, the Hebrew alphabet. Here, the decomposition necessary for an efficient representation takes place at the level of the spoken words which represent the concepts. The words are decomposed into subunits called phonemes each representing a different sound. The symbols or characters of the alphabet then represent the phonemes and it is their ordering that gives the meaning to the words. In this representation the primitives do not relate to concepts directly. There are 24 characters or primitives in this representation and we see that this is a much more efficient way of attaching symbols to concepts.

Is there an analogy in the vision world...? Well it would be nice to be able to use the principle of decomposition and to invent some form of shape primitives. One way would be to decompose the image into short line segments each with a particular orientation. This is called **chain coding** . Chain codes provide a representation of shape that is a function of the gradient of the boundary of the shape.

In its simplest form, chain coding allows the boundary contour to be approximated by a sequence of horizontal, vertical and diagonal steps in the following way. Some

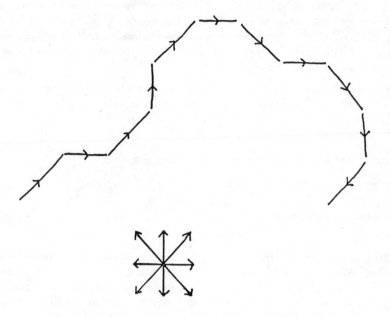

Fig 1.6 *Chain coding approximation of a curve*

arbitrary starting point on the boundary curve is chosen. For each point of intersection of the shape boundary with a grid line, the nearest point of the grid is included in the encoding of the boundary shape. When the constituent segments are joined together they form a polygonal arc which is then an approximation to the shape boundary, see Fig. 1.6 . The arc is called a chain and can be completely specified by a starting point and the sequence of directions necessary to follow the chain. Thus, an alphabet of shape with eight primitives is provided, these are then processed by techniques from formal language theory. See references [Shaw 1969], [Pavlidis et al 1979] and [Fu 1982].

The properties of chain codes can be easily derived and used in defining shape, see Freeman, [Freeman 1974]. Properties made explicit by the technique are, the Euclidean length of the chain, the maximum cross sectional length in any of the given 8 orientations and the first moments in any of those orientations. However, chain coding in its simplest form means that important information about curvature may be lost because of the coarse discretization of the curve. A generalization of the chain coding technique allows for arbitrary lengths and directions of chain elements [Freeman H. 1979]. In general the shape boundary is segmented into pieces described by arbitrary functions, these are usually restricted to low order polynomials.

Many algorithms exist for the piecewise linear approximation of boundaries, of these the most notable are Pavlidis [Pavlidis 1973], [Pavlidis et al 1975], [Ramer 1972],

11

Rosenfeld [Rosenfeld et al 1973] and Davis [Davis 1977]. The procedure may be divided into two types. The first attempts to find the lines directly. This is done by searching for boundary segments which are well fitted by lines. The second attempts to find the break points directly. This is done by searching for boundary points with locally high values of curvature. Thus points of maximum curvature on the boundary are used to generate polygonal approximations. If intermediate values of the curvature of the boundary are important then splines may be used to give better approximations to the boundary.

We seem to be doing quite well in our quest for a good representation of shape but let's double check, let's take another look at the Hebrew alphabet. Haven't they left something out?

It seems that they have left quite a few things out...

All of the vowels in fact...

Hebrew is a system of writing called a consonantal system. Only the consonants are written. When the words are vocalized this has to be done in the context of the particular text. The primitives of the representation therefore need proping up in a very substantial way with the help of dots and bars called diacriticals that tell you how to pronounce the word correctly.

So have we, as in the case of Hebrew, left something out? Yes we have, chain coding gives us insufficient information about the spatial relationships between the segments that would correspond to our perception of shape. The weakness inherent in this and other curve approximation schemes is that since the representation is one dimensional, the shape of the interior region is not made explicit. That is, such methods make explicit the relationships between adjacent points along the contour but do not make explicit where and in what ways the contour doubles back on itself. This doubling back has a marked effect on our concept of shape and is discussed by Latto et al. in their paper, *The Representation of Shape* [Latto et al 1984]. An example is shown in Fig. 1.7 . The two quite dissimilar shapes can be constructed from a dozen line segments with almost identical slopes. Whereas *locally* pieces of the two contours may be very similar, small changes in the slopes greatly affect the area enclosed by the contour and the notional shape it creates.

The problems concerning shape representation using the above methods arise because the data structures which derive from them are one dimensional whereas, shape is inherently a two dimensional attribute. We have gathered another essential property:

4.) **Geometric and Spatial Relations**
It is not sufficient to decompose the image into its constituent shape primitives, in addition, the representation should also make explicit the geometric and spatial relations between those shape primitives

12

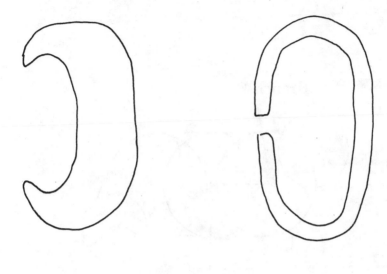

Fig 1.7 *Comparing dissimilar shapes*

What then is a good alphabet? The **ROMAN ALPHABET** is a pretty good alphabet. Its primitives (or characters) are efficient and there are sufficient of them to represent the sound system they code without the aid of other forms of representation. So far we have been well served by our analogy to writing systems. From it we have learned that a good representation of shape might be one that requires that an object be decomposed into components or primitives. A representation may then be constructed as a frame or net that expresses the links between primitives. These ideas have been made explicit in two important papers by Marr et al., [Marr et al 1978] and Minsky, [Minsky 1975]. In particular Biedermann, [Biedermann 1985] has produced a theory of qindexBiedermann recognition by components *Recognition By Components*, RBC. Biedermann's model suggests that the object is initially segmented into components each labelled using a limited set of component shapes and recognition is based on the topological and geometric relationships between components. He has shown by experiment that, for human subjects, line drawings are adequate stimuli for object recognition and that recognition still occurs when incomplete or degraded line drawings are presented.

Let's move on now and look at some other theories of shape detection that do not fit so neatly into our analogy. The first of these are **Axial representations**. Classes of *ribbon-like* planar shapes can be defined by specifying an arc, called a spine or axis, and a geometric figure, such as a disc or line segment, called the generator, that sweeps out the shape by moving along the spine, changing size as it does so. Various axial representations exist most notably, the **Medial (symmetric) Axis Transform** . This method was first proposed by Blum, [Blum 1967].

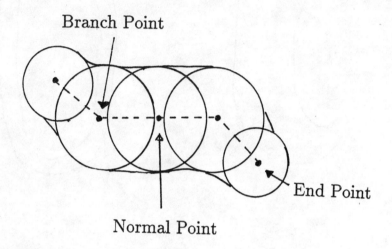

Fig 1.8 *The medial axis transform*

The medial axis transform has major disadvantages; the boundary of an object is a much more economic representation than its spine or skeleton; branch points give a poor response where there is a discontinuity on the boundary contour of the shape and the representation does not produce readily identifiable primitives.

Brady, [Brady 1982], [Brady M.J. et al 1984] has analysed the shortcomings of the medial (symmetric) axis transformation and has introduced an alternative region based representation, **Smoothed Local Symmetries** . This method combines features of the medial (symmetric) axis transformation and two dimensional generalized cylinders. An algorithm has been developed to execute this method, [Brady et al 1984]. In order to detect the Smoothed Local Symmetries tangent directions are computed using the Canny edge detector [Canny 1983]. These values are then used to detect significant changes of curvature along the bounding contour of the shape. Curvature changes are not recorded as single points but rather grouped to produce an effect or event. Examples of the curvature primitives used by Brady are, the corner, the crank and the bump or dent. Thus an added feature of this method is that the curvature change events may be used as primitives in a contour based representation of shape.

14

Such a description is referred to as *The Curvature Primal Sketch* , [Asada et al 1986]. and is analogous to Marr's primal sketch, [Marr 1980]. In the second stage of the processing, the shape is approximated by best fitting straight lines and circles to the feature points found in the first stage. The final stage is to use the Smoothed Local Symmetries to match a database of shape models for recognition and inspection.

This method of computing and representing shape has much to recommend it, not least because it exists as a hybrid of both region and contour based methods; it generates perceptually meaningful primitives and it has been shown to be computationally realistic. The major disadvantage of the method is that the generation of the axes of symmetry is not a straight forward process and it is not easy to specify how to define the set of generators.

There are further methods which do not map so well onto our previous conceptions about symbolic representations. This is because they are dependent upon mathematical operations which are not intuitively obvious. Nevertheless they are important and should be discussed.

One of the most important of these methods is the **method of moments** . Using this technique, shape is considered to be a global property of the image. Global invariants are sought by taking a double integral over the image. See references [Hu 1962] and [Duda et al 1973.]. The method provides for recognition of shapes independent of scaling, translation or rotation. Definitions and properties of moment invariants under translation, scaling, orthogonal, linear transformations and general linear transformations are developed. It is the moment invariants and not the moments themselves which serve as the descriptive elements in the representation of shape.

While much work has been done in this area using real, noisy data, it remains unproven that any global shape invariants can be detected from such integrals [Casasent et al 1984]. Target recognition in terms of moment invariants is handicapped by the interdependence of different orders due to the requirements of dilation and intensity invariance. Its compensation requires accurate moment evaluation. In addition, targets having an irregular structure require the computation of high order moments for recognition, making the design of discriminators complicated. More importantly, where a shape is partially occluded, then the moments of the resulting image are radically different from those of the unoccluded shape. We meet yet another criterion in our quest for a good representation of shape:

5.) **Similarity**
To be useful for recognition, the similarity between two shapes must be reflected in their descriptions but at the same time the representation should also encode subtle differences, [Brady 1984]

Transform methods are another class of mathematical techniques. One of the best known of these is the **Fourier Transform** . Using this method, the boundary of a two dimensional shape can be represented in terms of the gradient of the boundary as a function of arc length, see [Zahn et al 1972], or as a complex parametric function, see [Granland 1972]. In both cases the function is periodic and may be expanded in a Fourier series. The shape may be parametrized to any degree of accuracy by retaining a sufficient number of terms in the series.

Fourier transform methods are, at first sight, an attractive method of defining shape; the theory is highly developed and much well tested software exists; Fourier shape models can be made rotation, translation and scale invariant. However, the technique has two major disadvantages. In common with the method of moments, it characterizes global features well but the local features of a shape may be difficult to describe without taking many terms in the Fourier series. Similarly occlusion or agglomeration may produce coefficients unrelated to those of the original shape. The method of moments and fourier coefficients share an additional fundamental deficiency. The global features they compute are an inefficient way of characterising shape. It may be that a shape is immediately recognizable from some local feature that sets it apart from other shapes. We gather yet another necessary item for our list:

6.) Saliency
The representation should be such that gross or salient features associated with shape can be made explicit and used to bring essential information to the foreground allowing smaller and more easily manipulated descriptions to suffice, [Biedermann 1985].

Once again we see that the capacity to decompose a shape into irreducible shape primitives is a fundamental prerequisite of any representation of shape. Contour-based representations generally lend themselves more favourably to the generation of shape primitives. However, while contour-based methods do have the advantage of generating perceptually meaningful primitives they still have one major disadvantage in that it is generally necessary to employ curve following techniques to extract information about the primitives and hence such methods are very sensitive to discontinuities in the edge image data such as might be caused by noise or poor contrast. In consideration of this we can deduce one final criterion for a good representation of shape:

7.) Stability
It is important, at the low levels of computation, to ensure that access to the representation of an object does not depend on absolute judgements of quantitative detail.

This is a very fundamental prerequisite because the processes leading to the formation of a representation will nearly always concern a transition from events in the real world which are described by noisy, continuous data. This may involve thresholding responses whereby essential as well as incidental information may be lost. Such problems may be solved in the case of contour-based shape primitives by using the image processors' technique of the transformation of edge image data into a parametric transform space. Using this technique, shapes are characterized by the parameters associated with the curves that form the boundary of the object. The spatially extended data of the binary edge image of the object are transformed to produce spatially compact features in a suitable parameter space.

The most widely used parametric transformation method is the **Hough transform** technique. This has many *aficionados* and the literature is full of innovative implementations. An up-to-date and comprehensive review of the use of the Hough transform is given by Illingworth and Kittler [Illingworth et al 1987]. It is not appropriate to give an in depth description of the method at this point in the text. What follows is simply a short description of the method and the advantages it presents with respect to shape detection. The reader is given a much fuller treatment in the chapters that follow.

Originally, the Hough transform [Hough 1962] was used to detect straight line segments in digital images. The method is usually applied to an edge image , i.e. a binary or thresholded description of the edges in the original image. A line segment in the image space may be represented by a pair of quantized parameters. The complete set of possible lines for the whole image can be represented by an accumulator array whose axes are the parameters characterizing the line. Thus for each (x_i, y_i) edge image point the accumulator array is incremented for every possible line through the point (x_i, y_i). If many edge responses lie on the same line then this results in a high value at the position in the accumulator array corresponding to that line.

The Hough transform is classed as a method of performing efficient binary convolutions of the shape model with the edge image. We will investigate what this means in some detail in the chapters that follow. Let's see what's in store by re-examining our list of criteria necessary for a good representation of shape.

1. **Decomposition** We will demonstrate in chapter two that the Hough Transform is able to decompose a binary edge image or contour map into its constituent shape primitives. In addition it is not necessary for the object under detection to be segmented from a scene before detection can take place.

2. **Invariance** We will see in chapter five that the representations of shape developed using the Hough Transform can be made independent of scale, rotation and translation and that the viewer-object correspondence can be recovered.

3. **Accessibility** The development of fast, efficient implementations of parametric transformation methods of shape detection has received much attention in the recent literature. In chapter six we will review these techniques which show that it is possible to implement the Hough Transform in a time commensurate with real time applications, e.g. at video rates.

4. **Geometric and Spatial Relations** Parametric transform methods facilitate the building of a good representation of shape. We see in chapter five that the geometric and spatial relationships associated with the primitives of a contour-based representation may be readily deduced using the values of the parameters made explicit by the transformation.

5. **Similarity** Before the problem of similarity can be addressed it is necessary to make available a symbolic representation of the shape under detection. In chapter five it

will be shown that symbolic descriptions of shape can be derived quite naturally using the Hough Transform technique to make explicit the parametric information associated with the primitives of the representation.

6. **Saliency** In chapter five we see that Hough Transform methods can be used to extract two or three salient primitives from an edge image and this means that objects can be quickly recognised even when they are partially occluded or their images are extensively degraded.

7. **Stability** With respect to the Hough transform technique, the existing work is such that the robustness of the technique in the presence of noise and extraneous or incomplete data has been demonstrated. In chapter six we review the theory concerning the performance of the method.

From the above we can see that the Hough Transform has much to recommend it as a method of shape detection.

CHAPTER 2

Transforms Without Tears

In the previous chapter we have considered shape detection per se and have decided (with a little biased guidance!) that parametric transformation is a good way of partitioning points on the boundary of a shape (Edge Image Data) into sets. Each set is then labelled by the parameters associated with the shape formed by those points. In order to be able to put such a theoretically powerful technique to good use it is necessary not just to 'know' about it but to understand it in a way that enables it to be implemented and manipulated to best advantage. However, the process of integral transformation is not an intuitively obvious one. Difficulty in visualizing the transformation process and its results may be compounded in that the intended user may not feel happy or safe handling sophisticated mathematical concepts. It is to these people that this chapter is addressed.

The process of developing the theory is taken in two stages. The first stage consists of unashamedly simple, wholey pictorial explanations aimed at developing a strong intuitive understanding of the process of parametric transformation without recourse to any mathematical skills. The second stage tackles the necessary maths using the same common sense approach. Intuitive insights gained in the first stage are used to illustrate the compact mathematical notation associated with the technique.

2.1 Beginning to See

Where should we start? What we have is raw image data. What we want is some way of recognising things in that image. We are now entering the world of the black box. What happens when professionals enter this world is that they enter at different points according to their particular disciplines. The image processing people come from the bottom up. They enter at the low level processing stage doing things like edge detection. The psychologists are top down people. They enter at the high level stages suggesting things like relational data structures. What they both succeed in doing is to create black boxes within black boxes (see Fig. 2.1).

The result is that often the end user may feel completely overwhelmed by the experts. He is unable, because of lack of training, to understand the contents of particular black boxes but, out of necessity, must string perhaps several of them together.

Let's forget these problems for a moment and try the ultimate bottom up approach. To invent our own vision system. Where do we start? A first requirement might be just to tell the difference between light and dark. In fact many simple organisms survive with just this most basic of vision systems. They have the beginnings of intelligent decision making based on visual information. We can replicate this with a photodetector which is a charged couple device (CCD) which converts light energy or intensity into an electrical signal.

Being able to tell light from dark is not going to get us very far. So what if we had lots of CCD's? We could arrange them into a uniform array and we would have something called a CCD camera. From such a camera we would get a digital image. This is an image that consists of many small pieces or picture elements called pixels (see Fig. 2.2).

Such an image is discretized both in terms of its spatial co-ordinates, (x, y) and its brightness or intensity, $I(x, y)$. In Fig. 2.2 we see the image of a disc. It is a binary image, i.e. there are only two values the intensity can take, in this case, zero or one corresponding to off or on. The image is shown in two different forms. The black and white intensity map, shown as an inset, is the kind of representation we are most familiar with. In addition a surface plot of the intensity map is shown. This illustrates more clearly the discrete nature of the image.

Now we have an image but how can we extract information concerning shape from that image? Let's try the simplest of arithmetic operations, counting. We could just count and in that way we could tell from the number of 'on' pixels the size of thing we are looking at. However, things rarely appear in isolation just for our convenience and we need to know much more than size. What would happen if we employ a slightly more sophisticated counting system and kept running totals of the number of 'on' pixels column by column? That is we probe or test each column in turn for

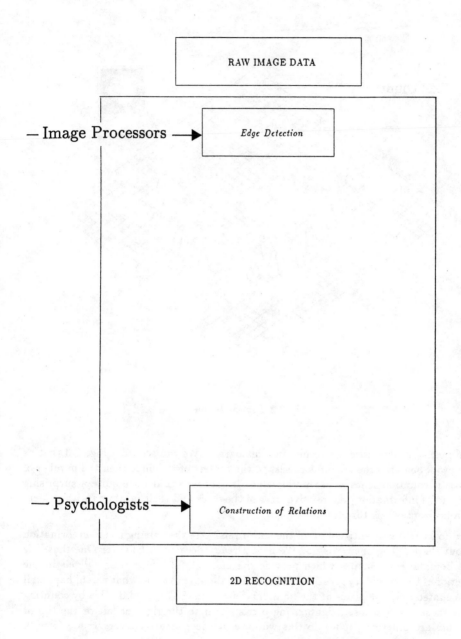

Fig 2.1 *Black Boxes within Black Boxes*

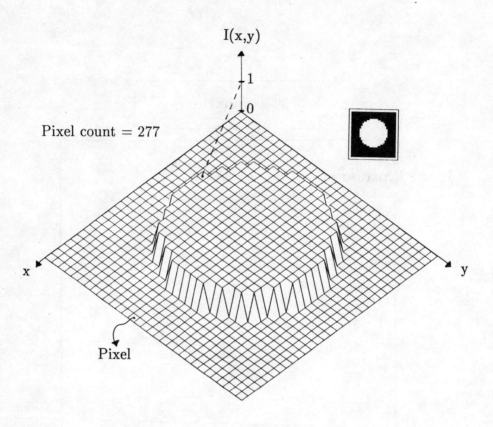

Pixel count = 277

Fig 2.2 *Digital Image*

'on' pixels and we store the results in a histogram. We can see from Fig. 2.3 that as the probe searches the columns closest to the centers of the discs then the number of pixels it counts reaches a maximum value. In fact we can deduce quite a surprising amount of information, the relative sizes of the discs and their positions with respect to a horizontal axis through the image.

But do we really need to count all the 'on' pixels? Are they giving us any information about shape? The answer is no. We have already decided in Chapter One that it is the boundaries of shapes which provide the most useful information. Pixels in the interior of the boundary give little information about shape. So what would happen if we counted only the pixels at the boundary of a shape? We could do this by counting only those pixels whose neighbouring pixels either to the right or left or the top or bottom are different. If we do this we have in effect created a very crude form of edge detection.

When we use this new way of counting we are getting maximum pixel counts when the probe first meets the circle left by our edge detection process (see Fig. 2.4).

22

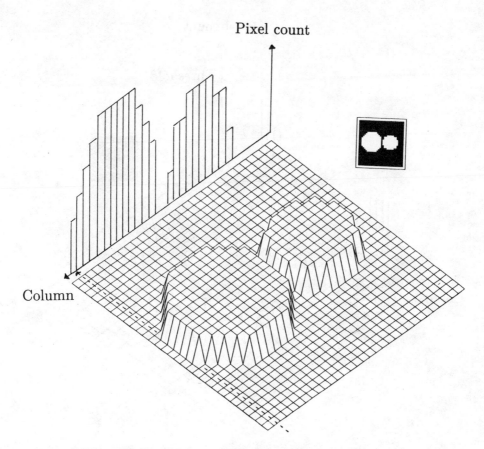

Fig 2.3 *Counting 'ON' Pixels Column by Column*

Two maxima occur. These are at the tangential positions of the probe as it meets the discrete image of the circle. From this information it's possible to deduce the diameter of the circle and its position with respect to the horizontal axis through the image by simply locating the maxima. At this stage such an operation is very simple, we can threshold, rejecting those values below our chosen threshold and accepting those above.

However, there is a lot more to appreciate here. We can see that we have the power to represent the image to any degree of resolution by simply dividing our image into smaller and smaller pieces. We can see the effect of making the pixel size smaller in Fig. 2.5 . In fact we could make the pixel size approach zero and maxima would still appear at the tangential positions of the probe or now, more properly, the probe line. We have what the mathematicians would call a limiting case and we could, if we so desired write an analytical equation to describe this process of transforming edge image data into something parametric with which we are able to label shapes. But let's not get ahead of ourselves. If we take a closer look at Fig. 2.5 we see that the

23

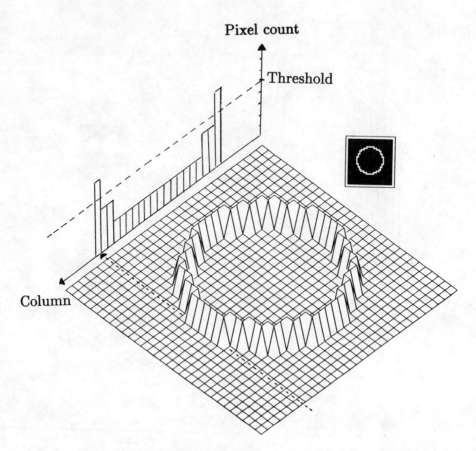

Fig 2.4 *Counting only pixels on the Boundary*

circle has been displaced in the vertical direction but we have no way of telling this from the information extracted by counting. The distribution of maxima is exactly as if the circle were still situated centrally in the image. This has happened because we are functioning in only one dimension. We have no access to information concerning the y direction of the image. We need to expand our counting process to deal with this extra dimension. We can do this by rotating our probe line and keeping a check with respect to each angular displacement, θ, and each radial displacement, p. See Fig. 2.6 .

To do this we make a new histogram for each angular displacement. We then stack them in their proper order and in so doing create a two dimensional space in which to store the information derived from counting. Each slice through this space tells us the way in which the pixel count varies with p for a single fixed value of θ. We now have a two dimensional parametric transform space, see Fig. 2.6 . Intensity maps of the binary image and the transform space are shown as insets. The transform space is also shown as a surface plot. If we consider the value p to have a direction, either

24

Pixel count

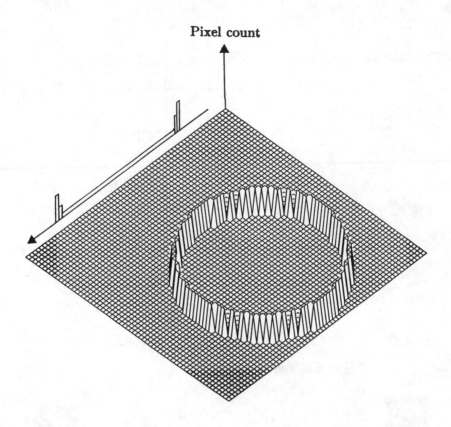

Fig 2.5 *Making the Pixel size smaller*

positive or negative, as well as a length then we need only consider θ in the range $[0, \pi]$ and p will be in the range $[p, -p]$ as shown. That is, over the semi-circular arc $[0, \pi]$, p is positive and then any further revolution of the probe line causes p to become negative.

2.2 What about Shape?

Are we any nearer to our goal of shape detection? Let's take stock of what we've done. We can see that each tangent to our circle gives rise to a maximum value in the transform space. These tangents are parametrized by the (p, θ) values associated with the location of the maxima they generate in the transform space. If we were to threshold and then to locate these maxima we could use their (p, θ) values to create lines in image space. The circle could then be reconstructed from the envelope of its tangents as shown in Fig. 2.7 .

25

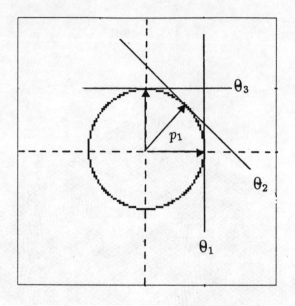

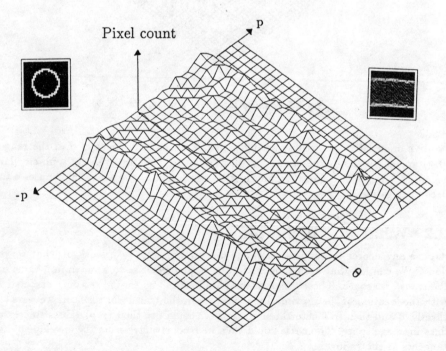

Fig 2.6 *Going into Two Dimensions*

26

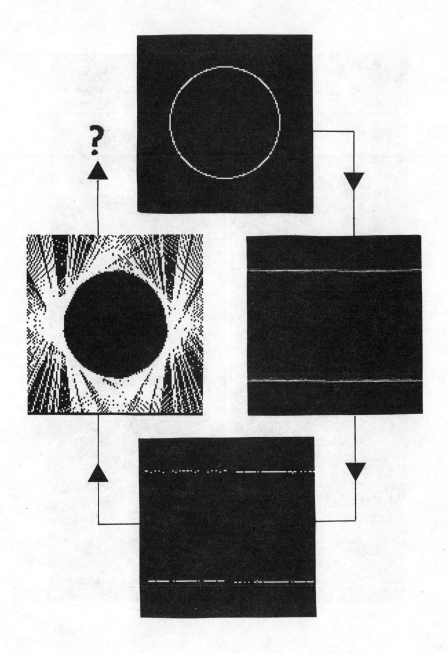

Fig 2.7 *Reconstruction from Tangents*

27

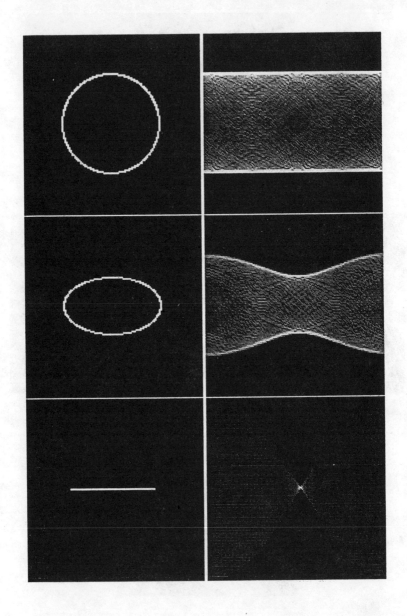

Fig 2.8 *Birth of a Butterfly!*

But what does all of this tell us about shape? The answer is, not much. We have arrived at a method of reconstruction rather than of shape detection. We can see that there is parametric information about the circle in that the distance between the two rows of maxima will tell us the diameter of the circle but this information is implicit, that is we would have to do some extra work to get at it. The only parametric information made explicit by our process relates to the tangents to the shape.

Maybe circles were a bit complicated to start with. Let's see if we can't make things simpler. Let's squash our circle. First we'd get an ellipse but if we went on squashing for long enough we'd get a straight line. If we now look at Fig. 2.8 we see that the effect in transform space is to produce a kind of butterfly feature with only one maximum value at the apex. That is to say that the straight line has only one tangent to itself. This looks much more promising!

If we now use the same counting or transformation process but our image contains straight lines we see from Fig. 2.9 that for each straight line in image space we get a maximum value appearing in the transform space at the (p, θ) co-ordinates that parametrize the straight line in image space. What is happening is that the probe line counts the number of image points which are coincident with it at a particular position and stores that information at the relevant (p, θ) location in transform space. For example, in Fig. 2.9 we see that the probe line at position $(p_{50}, \theta_{\pi/4})$ is coincident with a line. It therefore counts 70 image points on that line. It then stores this value of 70 at the point $(50, \pi/4)$ in the transform space.

What we have done with our counting process is to take information concerning the spatial co-ordinates, (x, y), of the image points and to transform it into a (p, θ) space from which information can be extracted in a very compact form. That information concerns the grouping of the points in image space into particular forms, straight lines. Thus a tremendous amount of spatially extended information in the binary image is transformed into just a few points, identified as local maxima, in the transform space. We are now able to decompose our image into its irreducible component parts or shape primitives, straight lines. The information made explicit by the transformation relates directly to the shape under detection. In addition, it is possible with very little extra effort to extract information implicit in the transformation process. We can tell which lines are parallel because they will have the same value of θ. We can tell how long the line is from the value of the pixel count at the point (p, θ). Remembering the criteria, for a good representation of shape, listed in Chapter One. These points are very much in keeping with criteria 1 and 4, those of decomposition and geometric and spatial relations.

It seems that a lack of mathematical skills does little to inhibit the capacity to invent a way of extracting information about shape from our image. Maybe now we are ready to look at the maths with some common sense insights to help us along.

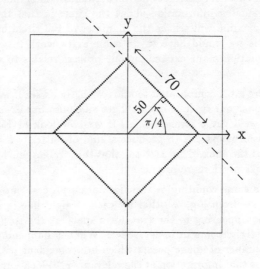

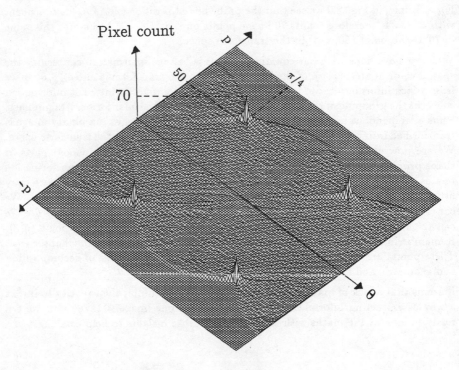

Fig 2.9 *Transforming straight lines*

2.3 Tackling the Maths

What we've done quite intuitively and with only the most basic of mathematical skills is to re-invent something called an integral transform which usually looks like this:

$$H(p,\theta) = \int\limits_{-\infty}^{\infty} \int\limits_{-\infty}^{\infty} I(x,y)\delta(p - x\cos\theta - y\sin\theta)\,dx\,dy \qquad (1)$$

Pretty fancy maths! Don't worry, all it is saying is exactly what we've been doing. Let's see how it is doing that by decoding the notation. Parametric transformation in the present context is usually called the Hough Transform and this is what the $H(p,\theta)$ notation refers to. It represents the value at a point, (p,θ), in the transform space and corresponds to what we have been calling the pixel count. Paul Hough, [Hough, U.S. Patent application 1962], deduced the method in order to detect the straight line tracks left by charged particles in a bubble chamber. He did this in pretty much the same way as you and I have just done, without any elegant maths, just some basic insight. In the 1970's other people began to get interested and to investigate the method, in particular Duda [Duda et al 1972] introduced the (p,θ) parametrization. In addition it was pointed out by Stanley Deans [Deans 1981] that the Hough Transform was in fact a special case of a more general transform, the Radon Transform [Radon 1917]. This transform had been around for half a century already and much theoretical work existed in the mathematical literature, for example see [Gel'fand et al 1966]. It was at this time that the Hough transform began to be written in the form of equation (1) .

What about the δ-function? What does it mean? Understanding the δ-function is fundamental to understanding parametric transformation. However, this very respectable looking function is not a mathematical function at all. Ideas concerning its behaviour have been current for over a century. Perhaps its most famous proponent was the physicist, Paul Dirac. It was he who first introduced the current δ-function notation in 1947[Dirac P.A.M. 1947]. In doing this he caused quite a controversy! So strong were the objections to this 'function' that Dirac was reduced to coining the term 'improper function'[Bracewell R.M. 1965]. What this means is that the integral of equation (1) is not a meaningful quantity until some convention for interpreting the δ-function is declared. Let's see what all the fuss was about.

If we think of a rectangle whose area is always 1, i.e. the product of its height, h, and its width, w is always equal to 1, we get the situation seen in Fig. 2.10 . If we make the width, w, smaller and smaller, such that it approaches zero, we see that the height, $h = 1/w$, would become correspondingly larger and larger until the rectangle resembled an infinitely tall spike with an infinitely thin width. This is normally represented as a line with an arrow on top, as shown.

If we imagine that this spike is situated at some point a along the x axis then we can describe the spike, using the δ-function notation, as:

$$\delta(x - a) = 0 \qquad (2)$$

for all $x \neq a$

That is the δ-function only exists at the point $x = a$. At all other places it simply does not exist. At the point a, the value inside the brackets of the δ-function, its argument, $x - a$, is 0. Therefore $\delta(0)$ is the only thing that we need to worry about.

31

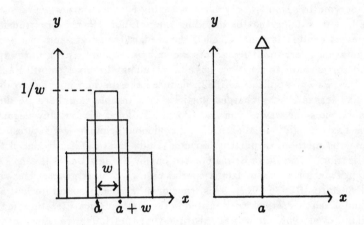

Fig 2.10 *Illustration of development of a δ-function*

Next we need to consider the fact that we are integrating something. In this case, the value of the integral of a function, $F(x)$, is just the area under the curve described by $F(x)$. So this one is easy! We already know that the area under this rather peculiar curve is 1. Hence we can write with great confidence:

$$\int\limits_{-\infty}^{\infty} \delta(x-a)\,dx = \int\limits_{-\infty}^{\infty} \delta(0)\,dx = 1 \qquad (3)$$

for $x = a$

Now comes the bit that makes the mathematicians mad! Consider an expression of the form:

$$\int\limits_{-\infty}^{\infty} F(x)\delta(x-a)\,dx \qquad (4)$$

as shown in Fig. 2.11 . What the δ-function does is to sample the function, $F(x)$, at the point $x = a$, effectively wiping $F(x)$ out at all other points. In this case the function, $F(x)$, can no longer take a variable value. It can have only the value at the point a, i.e. $F(a)$. It therefore behaves like a constant value and we can take it outside the integral to leave just the integral with respect to our $\delta(0)$ which we

32

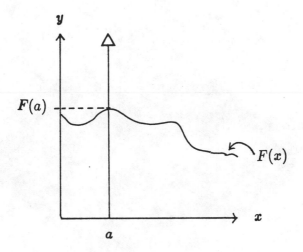

Fig 2.11 *Putting the δ-function to use*

already know is equal to 1 (from equation (3)). In this case the integral will then take the value of $F(a)$:

$$F(a) \int_{-\infty}^{\infty} \delta(0)\, dx = F(a) \qquad (5)$$

Couldn't be easier, but to the mathematicians of the day the Physicists' belief in the properties of the δ-function was little more than an act of faith! However, the δ-function has stood the test of time. It can be used to describe many physical systems characterized by impulses and it predicts results that can be validated by experiment.

How can we relate all of this to our δ-function? For a start ours is a lot more complicated. However, the same principle applies no matter how complicated things look. The δ-function only exists at those points where its argument is 0. This happens when

$$p = x \cos\theta + y \sin\theta \qquad (6)$$

and this is the equation describing the probe line we have been using in image space. We are now sampling our image along a line defined by equation (6) . It is as if we have an infinite number of one dimensional δ-functions constrained to be along a probe line of infinite length. See Fig. 2.12 Where the probe line and the image are

33

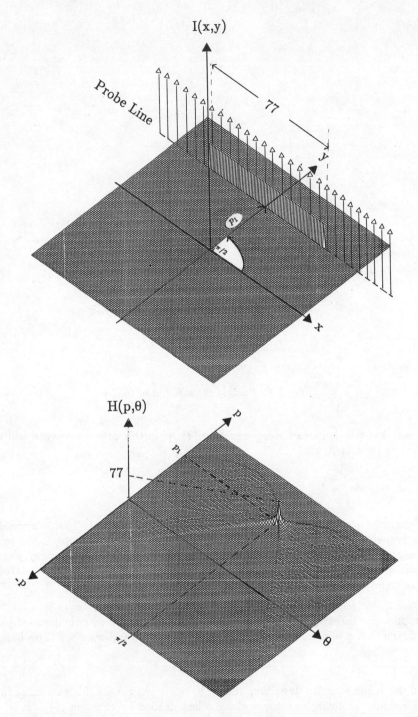

Fig 2.12 *p, θ Parametrization of the probe line*

coincident then the Integral simply sums all of the values of $I(x,y)$ at those points of coincidence. Again, this is easy. We have a binary image that is made up of only zeroes and ones. This means that the integral tells us the length of intersection of the probe line and the shape in the image just as we have seen using our intuitive method.

Now that we are a little further along the road to understanding this process of integral transformation let's consider another of the criteria for a good representation of shape listed in Chapter One, accessibility. Is what we propose computationally realistic?

2.4 Beginning to Compute

Before we begin to think about computing the transformation let's recapitulate what we have learnt about the maths. Referring to Fig. 2.12 :

1. The $I(x,y)$ term refers to the image intensity. This can be either 0 or 1.

2. The δ-function samples our image at all points where its argument is 0, i.e. along the line $p = x \cos \theta + y \sin \theta$.

3. The integral sign sums all values of the image intensity coincident with the probe line.

Everything exactly as we have been doing. So why do we need to bother with all this fancy maths? Physical intuition has taken us a long way but it is not the whole story. For example, using our intuitive method we would superimpose probe lines across our image and search along them for pixels having a value of one. We would then sum all of these values and place the result at the appropriate (p, θ) location in the transform space. In this way we would be doing little better then the one to one correspondence of template matching. Let's use the maths to see if there isn't a better way.

Considering item 2. above, we see that the transformation is only meaningful when image points (x,y) are solutions to the equation

$$p = x \cos \theta + y \sin \theta$$

and this is the way in which we can calculate the transformation efficiently. We know the values of x and y because they are simply the co-ordinates of the image points having a value of one. We therefore start by searching our image for a pixel having a value of one and spatial co-ordinates, (x,y). We can then use these values of (x,y) to calculate values of p for our range of θ. We do this by taking our $[0, \pi]$ range of θ and dividing it into equal pieces. In this way we end up with a list of θ values, θ_j, where the θ_j are evenly distributed along the interval $[0, \pi]$.

We can see what is happening if we now rewrite our defining equation in its discrete form:

$$p_j = x_i \cos \theta_j + y_i \sin \theta_j \tag{7}$$

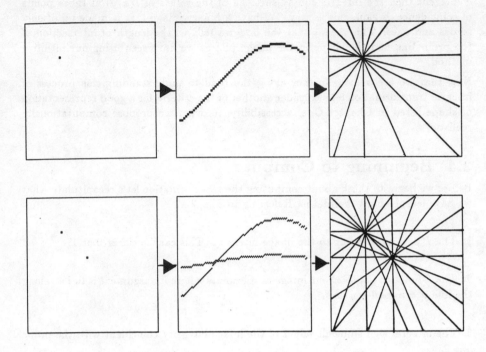

Fig 2.13 *Relating points to curves and back again*

The i, j subscripts refer to ordered pairs in the image and the transform space respectively. For every point, (x_i, y_i), of the image, i is fixed and the values p_j are calculated using stepwise increments of θ_j. Each calculated point, (p_j, θ_j), in the transform space is assigned a value of 1.

If we consider what this means we will see that it has been well worth doing the maths! Let's picture what is happening here. Each image point, (x_i, y_i), generates a cosine curve in transform space. Every point, (p_j, θ_j), on this curve specifies a line in image space that passes through the point, (x_i, y_i). See Fig. 2.13 . This is equivalent to placing many templates across the image but only where they will be most effective, that is where there is an image point. We do not need to consider this image point any further. We can discard it and take the next one. The difference between this and actual template matching is that the process is only activated by image points. Template matching requires a one to one correspondence check over all of the image irrespective of whether there are image points present or not. The present method is therefore much more efficient as was noted by Stockman[Stockman et al 1977].

If we process more image points then where the cosine curves they generate intersect, the function, $H(p, \theta)$, at the point of intersection will have a value equal to the number of intersecting curves. In this way each point is voting for all the possible lines that might pass through it and all of the votes are summed together to give us evidence of possible groupings of image points. We can then simply threshold to obtain the values of (p, θ) indicative of straight lines in the image space.

We have certainly come quite a long way in our quest of parametric transformation. We are now able to parametrize straight lines. We have done the maths and have begun to think about the computation. Maybe we should now think about entering the real world!

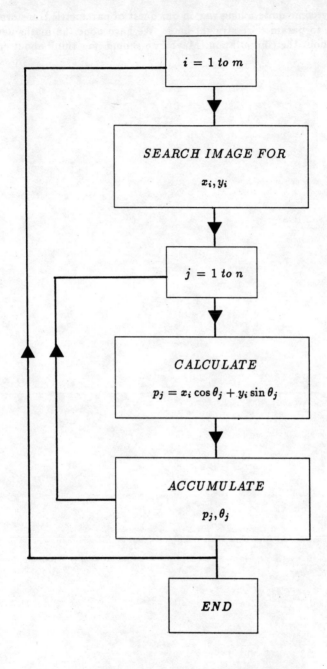

Fig 2.14 *Flow diagram of Hough Algorithm*

CHAPTER 3

Preprocessing

3.1 The Real World

In the previous chapter we have concerned ourselves with the basic theory of shape detection using parametric transformation. We have arrived at the point where we can confidently cope with straight line detection using computer generated binary data. In order to consolidate our position we will deal only with straight lines for the time being. This is because our next steps will bring us into head-on collision with the real world. This place is at one time noisy and packed full of confusing information. To begin with, a real image will not be conveniently binary. It will present itself as a two dimensional array of pixels or feature points each containing a discrete intensity value. The intensity values may vary over a relatively large range, for example [1, 256]. Some of the feature points will truly carry information about the real world. Others may have been corrupted in some unexpected way in the physical process of image acquisition. They are what we call noise.

When we start, we have no idea which of the feature points are of interest to us. We have to test each one in order to extract from the proliferation of information present in the raw image data, candidate feature points which may then be grouped into the perceptually meaningful units of straight lines. This is the bottom end of the shape detection processing hierarchy. It is what we have been calling 'low level' vision. In recent years much attention has been focused on these low level vision algorithms, for example edge detection and skeletonization. Much has been written about both of these topics. (See for example " Digital Image Processing'[Gonzalez et al 1987]. They are a very natural extension of image processing techniques, e.g. edge enhancement or image reconstruction. We will choose the algorithms best suited to our purpose of straight line detection.

In order to fully understand the process of edge detection it is necessary to develop some more mathematical tools. Don't worry, this will involve nothing more horrendous than multiplication and addition!

When we have extracted our edge image points there is one last thing we need to think about before we proceed. This is the question of which parametrization is best and why. In general, the decisions concerning suitable parametrizations are guided by the need for a realistic computational model. That is one which can be executed in a realistic time and make efficient use of computer memory. There are very many sophisticated algorithms designed to do this. We are not ready for them. They will be discussed in a later chapter. For the present we will content ourselves with implementing a straightforward algorithm. This will enable the reader to get a feeling for things such as Transform Space quantization without additional complications.

3.2 Spot the Difference

In chapter one we have decided that we are not interested in the interior regions of an object. These tell us very little about its shape. It is the feature points on the boundary of an object that give us the most information concerning shape. How do we set about identifying these points?

The real image of a wooden block is shown in Fig. 3.1 . A one dimensional cut has been made through the image along the line shown in black. The intensity changes occurring along this cut are shown in white. We can see that, taken together, the intensity values in the neighbourhood of the object's boundary contain very specific information. It is at these places that the intensity value varies the most. Looking at Fig. 3.1 we see that the background intensity from **A** to **B** varies little. The variations occurring may be due to random changes in the signal caused by the physical acquisition of the image. A large difference in the magnitude of adjacent intensity values occurs at **B**. This corresponds to the first edge of the block. From **B** to **C** the intensity values vary only slightly relative to each other with the trend being for the intensity to increase as the surface of the block comes closer to the viewer. If we look at the point **C**, we see that there is another very sharp change in the intensity. From **C** to **D** the intensity also slowly varies from point to point and the trend is for it to fall off as the block recedes in the field of view.

From the above considerations we should note the following. In detecting edges our task is to locate those feature points where the intensity changes are greatest with respect to the neighbourhood in which they are located. That is we are only

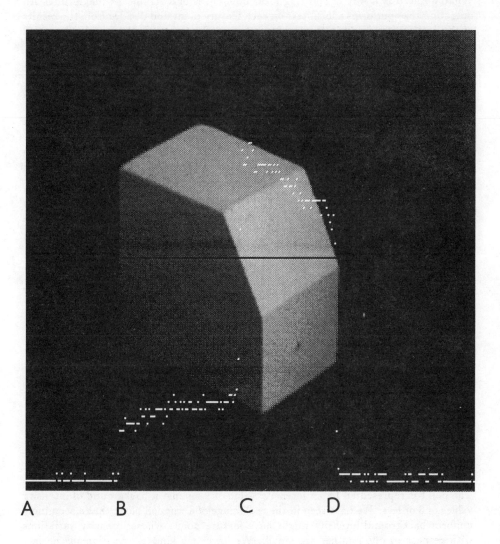

A   B   C   D

Fig 3.1 *Real Image of Wooden Block*

interested in local changes. It is no good to compare a value along the cut from **A** to **B** with a value along the cut from **B** to **C**, nor do we wish to respond to slowly varying intensity changes such as occur from **B** to **C**.

What we need is a way of spotting local differences of a significant magnitude: An operation that performs a local test on each feature point and decides from the results of the test whether or not the feature point is of interest. Let's consider how this might be done.

3.3 Convolution, a Necessary Tool

We are looking for changes in intensity which will alert us to significant feature points. Let's start by thinking about the simplest kind of object, a one dimensional point object. That is a point of relatively high intensity compared to its neighbours. For our purposes, a notional one dimensional point object may be represented as shown in Fig. 3.1 . It is an array of three intensity values where the central value is 2 and the values on either side are -1.

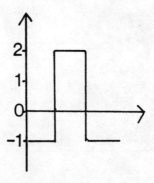

Fig 3.2 *Operator corresponding to notional point*

A one dimensional 'image' of a point object might be like the one shown in Fig. 3.3 . The point is represented by an intensity value of 9 against a background of intensity values of 3 or less. We have seen in the real image of a wooden block that a seemingly uniform background intensity might have feature points whose intensity variations with respect to one another are small. We have this kind of variation in the last element of the array. This value is 1 whereas the other background points have a value of 3. We therefore need to define some operation that will cope with such a variation without giving a significant response.

What we need to do is to take the distribution associated with a notional point and to somehow compare it with the distribution around each feature point and see where we get a match. In this sense we will operate on the image with the operator representing a notional point shown in Fig. 3.2 . We can do this by lining up the operator so that its central value of 2, representing the relatively high intensity value

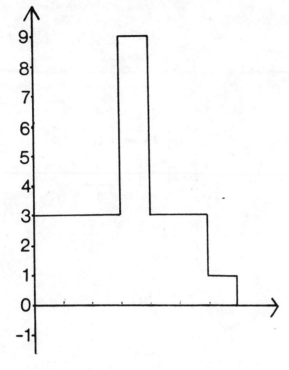

Fig 3.3 *One dimensional Image of a point object*

of a point object, coincides with our candidate feature point shown in a black square in Fig. 3.4 (a). We then proceed to multiply each value in the image array with the corresponding value in the operator as shown. The results of these multiplications are then summed and stored in a new array at the position corresponding to the position of the candidate feature point in the image. In this case the sum is zero. We therefore see that for a uniform distribution of intensity values, the response is zero.

If we continue shifting the operator so that it is coincident with each feature point in turn and we perform the same operation at each point as shown in Fig. 3.4 (a), (b) and Fig. 3.5 (a), (b), then we obtain a new array that tells us the responses at all points in the image except the two at the beginning and the end of the array. These points only have one nearest neighbour and therefore cannot be considered.

What does it all mean? Fig. 3.6 gives us a picture of what has happened. If we ignore the zero or negative responses we see that there is only one positive response to the operations we have just carried out over the image. The value at this point, (12), is large with respect to the range of intensities of the image, [1,9], and it occurs at the position of our point object, the intensity value of 9. Our operator has successfully identified the position of this point object and has coped with the small variation in the background.

43

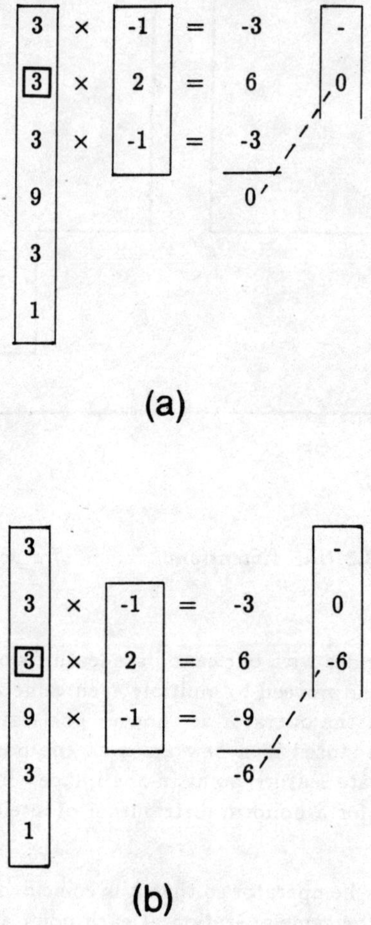

(a)

(b)

Fig 3.4 *Results of matching operator to image points*

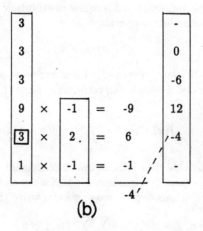

(a)

(b)

Fig 3.5 *Further results of matching operator to image points*

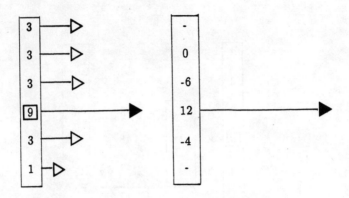

Fig 3.6 *Illustration of response to point detection operation*

The operation we have just described is called **convolution** [Bracewell 1965]. A shorthand notation for a convolution operation is:

$$I(x) \ * \ g(x) \tag{1}$$

We can therefore identify our image as $I(x)$ and our point operator as the convolution function, $g(x)$. In its one dimensional, continuous form the convolution operation is defined as:

$$I(x) * g(x) = \int\limits_{-\infty}^{\infty} I(a)g(x-a)\,da \tag{2}$$

The a is a dummy variable that tells us the displacement or shift of the convolution function, $g(x)$, with respect the function $I(x)$. If we wish to consider a discrete, two dimensional case such as our digital image we can write the convolution as:

$$I(x,y) * g(x,y) = \sum_{i}\sum_{j} I(i,j)g(x-i,y-j) \tag{3}$$

Convolution is a very necessary and important tool for many computer vision tasks. It cannot be skipped over. Readers who have done this should now go back and make certain they have understood the operation for the simple one dimensional case.

We have used the convolution operation to identify a particular distribution of feature points. In a similar way we can convolve the image with functions whose distribution matches that of a notional edge. In this case the convolution function is acting like a template.

3.4 Edge Detection

As we have said, the objective of an edge detection operation is to find the locations in the distribution of image data where the change in intensity is sufficiently large to be taken as a reliable indication of an edge. Edge operators differ in their sensitivity to different edge directions and in their sensitivity to noise. However, they all determine a direction which is aligned with the direction of the maximal change in grey levels. Methods of edge detection split into two camps. These are:

1. **Template Matching.** Following the method we have outlined above in the very simple one dimensional case, the image is convolved with templates of the edges under detection. Typically 12 masks are used to estimate the local components of the gradient in different directions.

2. **Differential Gradient approach.** This is similar to the template matching approach in that local intensity gradients are estimated with the aid of suitable convolution masks. However only two masks are needed, one for the x and y directions. The Differential Gradient approach is more computationally intensive than the template matching methods but gives more accurate results.

Interested readers will find a comprehensive review of edge detectors in reference [Davies 1990]. This is well worth consulting for it's clear and detailed discussions concerning edge detection operators.

We will use one of the most commonly used Differential Gradient edge detectors, the Sobel. This has two 3×3 masks, one for the x direction, M_x, and one for the y direction, M_y. These are each independently convolved with the image.

$$M_x = \begin{bmatrix} 1 & 0 & -1 \\ 2 & 0 & -2 \\ 1 & 0 & -1 \end{bmatrix} \quad M_y = \begin{bmatrix} -1 & -2 & -1 \\ 0 & 0 & 0 \\ 1 & 2 & 1 \end{bmatrix} \tag{4}$$

The results of performing these two convolution operations are then used to determine the magnitude of the edge, $mag(x,y)$ given by:

$$mag(x,y) = |M_x * I| + |M_y * I| \tag{5}$$

and the direction of the edge, $dir(x,y)$, given by:

$$dir(x,y) = \tan^{-1}\left(\frac{M_x * I}{M_y * I}\right) \tag{6}$$

Let's see how this works step by step using a simple image containing only one edge. The array of intensity values representing such an image is shown in Fig. 3.7 . In Fig. 3.7 , we see the edge operator for the x direction, M_x, centred on the element of the image array in the black square. Each element in the 3×3 square around the candidate feature point is multiplied by the corresponding element of M_x. The results are then summed. The sum is 0 because the image intensity does not vary

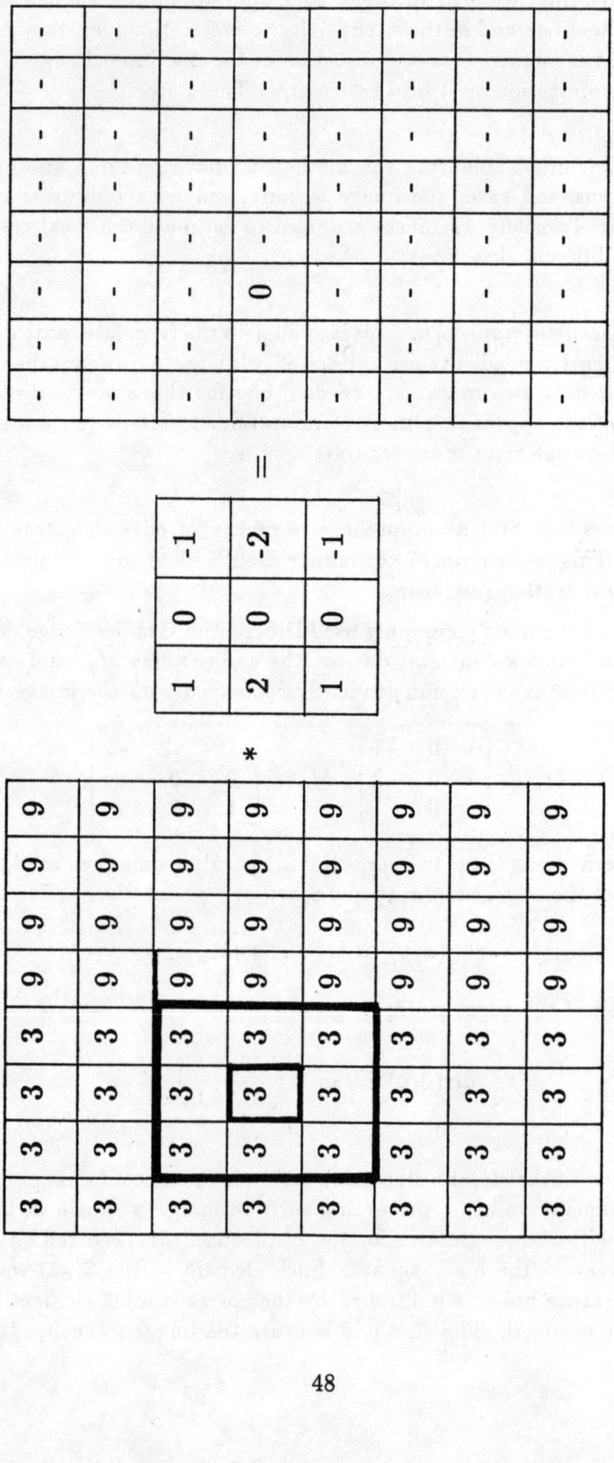

Fig 3.7 Convolving Sobel operator with uniform intensity pattern

$$
\begin{bmatrix}
3 & 3 & 3 & 3 & 3 & 3 & 3 & 3 \\
3 & 3 & 3 & 3 & 3 & 3 & 3 & 3 \\
3 & 3 & 3 & 3 & 3 & 3 & 3 & 3 \\
3 & 3 & 3 & 3 & 3 & 3 & 3 & 3 \\
3 & 3 & 3 & 3 & 3 & 3 & 3 & 3 \\
9 & 9 & 9 & 9 & 9 & 9 & 9 & 9 \\
9 & 9 & 9 & 9 & 9 & 9 & 9 & 9 \\
9 & 9 & 9 & 9 & 9 & 9 & 9 & 9
\end{bmatrix}
*
\begin{bmatrix}
1 & 0 & -1 \\
2 & 0 & -2 \\
1 & 0 & -1
\end{bmatrix}
=
\begin{bmatrix}
\cdot & \cdot & \cdot & \cdot & \cdot & \cdot & \cdot & \cdot \\
\cdot & \cdot & \cdot & \cdot & \cdot & \cdot & \cdot & \cdot \\
\cdot & \cdot & \cdot & \cdot & \cdot & \cdot & \cdot & \cdot \\
\cdot & \cdot & \cdot & 0 & \cdot & \cdot & \cdot & \cdot \\
\cdot & \cdot & \cdot & \cdot & \cdot & \cdot & \cdot & \cdot \\
\cdot & \cdot & \cdot & \cdot & \cdot & \cdot & \cdot & \cdot \\
\cdot & \cdot & \cdot & \cdot & \cdot & \cdot & \cdot & \cdot \\
\cdot & \cdot & \cdot & \cdot & \cdot & \cdot & \cdot & \cdot
\end{bmatrix}
$$

over the 3×3 neighbourhood around the candidate point. This 0 result is placed in an array of the same dimensions as the image and at the position of the candidate image point. In Fig. 3.8 we see the result of applying the convolution operation at a point that is positioned on the vertical edge in the image. This time the result is -24 as shown.

Fig. 3.9 shows the result of convolving each image point with the Sobel operator. We see that for the x direction there is a significant response of -24 along the direction of the edge in the image. The response spans two columns. Whereas the edge in the image is located between the fourth and fifth columns of the image array as shown in Fig. 3.9 , the detected edge is located between the two columns where the magnitude of the response to the convolution operation is highest. The response to the y direction operator would be 0 at all points in the image as there are no horizontal lines. Therefore the magnitude at each point labelled -24 in Fig. 3.9 is 24 and its gradient is given by:

$$dir(x,y) = \tan^{-1}\left(\frac{M_x * I}{M_y * I}\right) = \frac{-24}{0} = 90°$$

With our simple image we would be correct in assuming that an edge whose orientation was 90° to the horizontal was indeed located between the columns with values of -24 shown in Fig. 3.9 . However, a real image may not provide such good quality data. There may be some uncertainty in the location of candidate edge points and there may be some random corruption of the image data.

It is clear that the larger the mask, the more accurate the edge detection calculation and the less vulnerable is the operation to the effects of local noise. Larger masks do exist, but increasing the size of the mask causes a corresponding increase in computational effort and 3×3 operators are still the most popular. The optimal edge detector is a constantly debated theme in the literature. See, for example [Petrou M. 1988].

Fig. 3.10 shows the result of applying a 3×3 Sobel edge detector to the image of a block. This image is composed of the information concerning the magnitude of the edges. For our purposes of parametric transformation we need a binary image. We obtain this by thresholding. This is shown in Fig. 3.11 .

The threshold was chosen at 60% of the range of intensities of the Sobel image. The resulting binary image has some noise points. Such a moderate amount of noise would not degrade the results of the transformation process. However, it is computationally wasteful to transform such noise points. They are easily removed again using a 3×3 convolution operator [Gonzalez 1987]. The computational effort expended in this processing is easily traded off against the increase in speed when executing the transformation. Fig. 3.11 was cleaned up in this way.

The next thing to notice is that we have a characteristic band at the position of an edge. The image can be further improved by 'thinning' the bands such a way that they become single lines. A detailed thinning algorithm is given by Davies [Davies 1990] and was used to produce the image shown in Fig. 3.12 . We now have what Marr [Marr D. 1980] would call a primal sketch. That is an image devoid of information redundant to the process of shape detection. It is the input for the transformation process. Let's now pause to think how best to perform the transformation.

Convolution:

Image (8×8):

9	9	9	9	9	9	9	9
9	9	9	9	9	9	9	9
9	9	9	9	9	9	9	9
9	9	9	9	9	9	9	9
3	3	3	3	3	3	3	3
3	3	3	3	3	3	3	3
3	3	3	3	3	3	3	3
3	3	3	3	3	3	3	3

$*$

Sobel operator (3×3):

1	0	-1
2	0	-2
1	0	-1

$=$

Result (8×8):

'	'	'	'	'	'	'	'
'	'	'	'	'	'	'	'
'	'	'	'	'	'	'	'
'	'	'	'	'	'	'	'
'	'	'	-24	'	'	'	'
'	'	'	'	'	'	'	'
'	'	'	'	'	'	'	'
'	'	'	'	'	'	'	'

Fig 3.8 Convolving Sobel operator with edge point

50

-	0	-	-	-	-	-	-
-	0	0	0	0	0	0	-
-	0	0	0	0	0	0	-
-	-24	-24	-24	-24	-24	-24	-
-	-24	-24	-24	-24	-24	-24	-
-	0	0	0	0	0	0	-
-	0	0	0	0	0	0	-
-	-	-	-	-	-	-	-

=

1	0	-1
2	0	-2
1	0	-1

*

9	9	9	9	9	9	9	9
9	9	9	9	9	9	9	9
9	9	9	9	9	9	9	9
9	9	9	9	9	9	9	9
3	3	3	3	3	3	3	3
3	3	3	3	3	3	3	3
3	3	3	3	3	3	3	3
3	3	3	3	3	3	3	3

Fig 3.9 Convolving whole image with Sobel operator

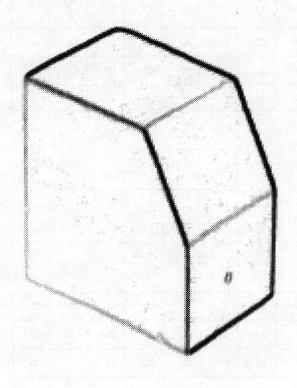

Fig 3.10 *Result of Sobel edge detection on real image*

Fig 3.11 *Result of thresholding Sobel image*

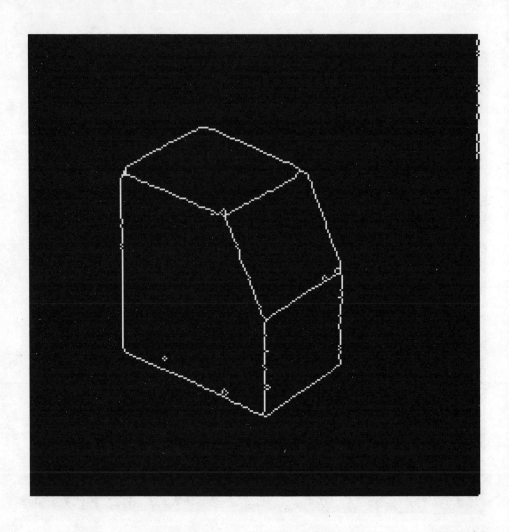

Fig 3.12 *Thinned image with noise points removed*

3.5 Which Parametrisation?

In chapter two a (p, θ) parametrisation of the straight line was introduced as part of an intuitive development of the ideas contained in parametric transformation. This is not the only possible parametrisation. We shall now consider other parametrizations and justify the use of the (p, θ) one in the present case. Three parametrizations will be discussed. These are the two most widely used and one of the more exotic variations for comparison.

The first parametrisation, that used by Hough in his original patent application [Hough 1962], uses the slope of the line, (a), and the intercept, (b), on the y axis to parameterise the line:

$$y = -ax + b \qquad (7)$$

The parameter space then becomes an (a, b) parameter space and the equation used to calculate the parameters is given by:

$$b_j = x_i a_j + y_i \qquad (8)$$

where the i and j subscripts refer to ordered pairs in the image and transform space respectively. As with the parametrization we have used, the transformation is accomplished by fixing i and calculating b_j over the range of a_j. Thus each point, (x_i, y_i), in image space will generate a straight line in the transform space. This is shown in Fig. 3.13 . Each point, (a_j, b_j), on the straight line in the transform space will code the parameters of a line passing through the point (x_i, y_i).

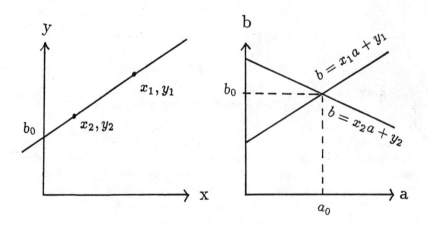

Fig 3.13 *Slope intercept parameterisation*

A major problem arises when using the slope intercept parametrisation in that both slope and intercept approach infinity as the line approaches a vertical position. This

55

problem is normally solved by using two accumulators for the transform space for example see [Kultanen 1990a]. Despite this difficulty the $y = mx + c$ parametrisation does offer some advantages in certain implementations and these will be discussed in a later chapter.

To overcome the problems associated with an unbounded parameter space, the second parametrisation, the normal parametrisation:

$$p = x \cos \theta + y \sin \theta \qquad (9)$$

was introduced by Duda and Hart [Duda et al 1972]. It is as shown in Fig. 3.14 . It is the one we have been using.

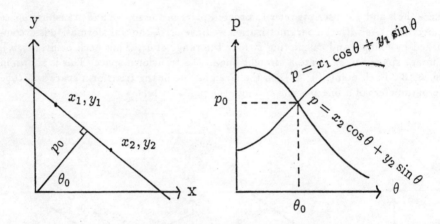

Fig 3.14 *Normal parametrization*

The line is defined by the (p, θ) parameters where p is the algebraic length of the normal to the line which also passes through the origin and θ is the angle that the normal makes with the x axis. As we have seen, each point, (x_i, y_i), in image space generates a cosine curve in the transform space. Each point, (p_j, θ_j), on that cosine curve codes the (p, θ) parameters of a straight line through (x_i, y_i). Thus the normal parametrisation overcomes the problems associated with an unbounded parameter space. This is the reason it has been chosen in the present case.

Other parameterisations exist, for example [Davies 1990], [Forman 1986], [Wallace 1985]. Of these the most well known is the Muff Transform [Wallace R.S. 1985]. Muff is a contraction of Modified Hough. It is a bounded straight line parametrisation that uses the two points of intersection of the projected line, as it cuts the perimeter of the image. See Fig. 3.15 .

56

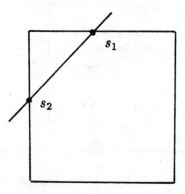

Fig 3.15 *Muff parametrization*

These are stored as two distances s_1 and s_2 along the outer edge of the image. The distance is measured in a counter clockwise direction and uses the lower left corner of the image as an origin. The representation can be made unique by applying the condition that $s_1 < s_2$. One major advantage of the method is that the resolution of the lines represented is uniform and matches exactly the set of lines which can be drawn across the image using digital graphics techniques.

3.6 Getting Started

To begin to implement an algorithm it is always best to have a flow diagram as a starting point. This means thinking out exactly what you are expecting the computer to do before you ask it to do it. This is where your program should start. Do not expect to program whilst sitting at the terminal. Never assume that your program is going to work first time! Have some easy test examples to run through it for the purpose of debugging.

The algorithm we will use is simple and quick to implement. It is not an efficient, 'computer-wise' algorithm but is suitable for the novice 'Hougher'. It can be used to generate the transformation and to get a feeling for the technique before any further complications are introduced. Fig. 3.16 shows a flow diagram of the algorithm.

From this we see that the image is represented as an $N \times N$ array, $I(N, N)$. The results of the transformation are accumulated in an array, $H(N, N)$. Before beginning the program proper we should calculate two arrays, $SIN\theta(N)$ and $COS\theta(N)$. This saves much computational effort when running the program proper as we do not need to repeatedly call up the values of $\cos\theta$ and $\sin\theta$. The first value of θ should be $-2 * \pi/n$. Why should this be? If we remember from chapter two that the cosine curves representing our transformed image are cyclic. We can represent all values uniquely with p and θ in the ranges $[-p, p]$ and $[0, \pi]$ respectively. The transform

57

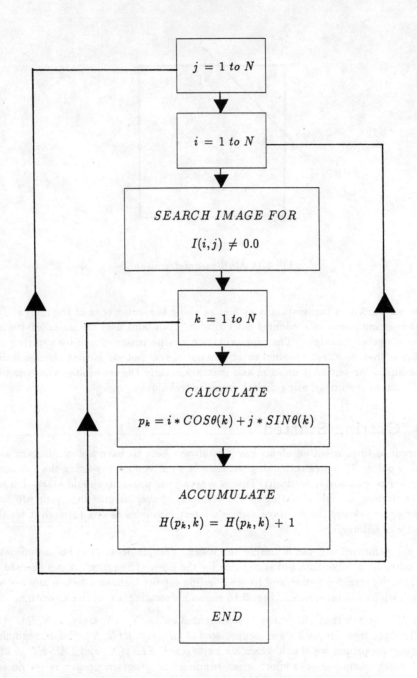

Fig 3.16 *Flow diagram of Basic Hough Algorithm*

plane thus has the topology of a Mobius strip. If it is twisted and joined at the ends it will form a continuous surface. This means that any value on the left of the representation of the transform plane that is displaced to the left will reappear on the right hand side of the transform plane with the sign of p reversed as shown in Fig. 3.17 .

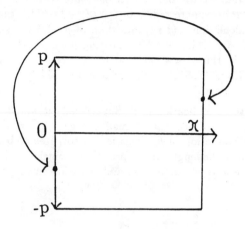

Fig 3.17 *Topology of transform plane*

In a real image there will be some uncertainty in the position of the image points and this will be reflected in the way in which the votes are distributed around a maximum value in the transform space. Vertical lines might be parameterised by a positive value of p and a value of $\theta = 0.0$. They may also, because of uncertainty in the data or perhaps due to rounding or truncation errors in the computing, be parametrized by a negative value of p and $\theta \geq 180.0$. We see in the next chapter that the search for maxima in the transform space will entail considering the distribution of votes around a point and not simply the number of votes at any single point. Because vertical lines are an important component of most images, it would not be wise to allow the splitting of votes that might occur if the first column in the array represented a value of $\theta = 0.0$. Hence the third column in the array is the column corresponding to $\theta = 0.0$.

The program proper begins when we search the array representing the image, $I(i,j)$, along each row, j, and each column, i. When we encounter an element, $I(i,j)$ that is not zero this is a feature point and we proceed with the transformation process. That is we calculate a value, p_k, corresponding to each of N values of θ. We perform the accumulation by incrementing the value of $H(p_k, k)$ by one.

3.7 Quantization

In the above implementation we have represented p in integer steps in the range $[-N/2, (N/2) - 1]$. That is, p is quantized in steps of $\Delta p = 1$. This matches the quantization of the image and assumes that the origin of the image is at its centre. What this means is that we will only detect lines intersecting a circle centred on the image and with an approximate radius of $((N/2) - 1)$. This makes life very much easier in terms of calculation and accumulation of p. All we need to do is to take the calculated value of p which will be a floating point number and to round it to the nearest integer. In this way a line that is one pixel thick will produce a single maximum value in Hough space. A line that is two pixels thick will produce two maxima at the same value of θ.

More interesting is the quantization in θ. Superficially it would appear that we can make the quantization in θ arbitrarily small and gain a corresponding increase in accuracy of the determination of θ. This is not so! Remember that the value of the transform is simply the length of the probe line coincident with the shape under detection. Let's take a very simple case and see what happens if we decrease the quantization steps in θ.

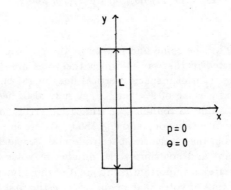

Fig 3.18 *Length of intersection of probe line*

In Fig. 3.18 we have a line, 1 pixel thick and of length L. If the probe line is parameterised by $p = 0.0$ and $\theta = 0.0$ then the length of intersection of the image line and the probe line will be $l = L$. If the probe line is then rotated about the origin by some angle $\delta\theta$, then two cases may result each depending on the quantization step $\Delta\theta$:

Case 1. The angle of rotation is such that the length of the probe line is greater than the length of the line under detection. Given that the difference in lengths cannot be resolved to an accuracy of less than 1 pixel then a value of L for the length of intersection will be recorded at this new value of $\theta = \Delta\theta$. That is the peak in transform space will split in the θ direction. This is precisely the case which should be avoided if digitized line segments are to be detected by the location of a single maximum in the transform space. This may be done by ensuring that

$$\delta\theta > \tan^{-1}\left(\frac{\delta r}{L}\right) \tag{10}$$

Case 2. If the condition given by equation (10) is true then the length of the probe line coincident with the image line is given by

$$l = \frac{\delta r}{\sin \delta\theta} \tag{11}$$

See Fig. 3.19

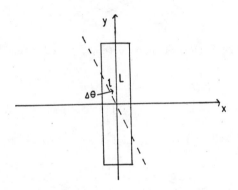

Fig 3.19 *Value of the integral for* $\delta\theta \geq \tan^{-1}\left(\frac{\delta r}{L}\right)$

By way of illustration, consider a line of length 32 pixels and width 1 pixel. i.e., $L = 32$. If the quantization steps in transform space are $\delta r = 1$ and a value of $\delta\theta > \tan^{-1}(\delta r/L)$ is chosen, the resulting transformation is as shown in Fig. 3.20 as a surface plot of the transform plane. If however, the value of $\delta\theta$ drops below $\tan^{-1}(\delta r/L)$, then the result is as shown in Fig. 3.21. An isolated maximum value is not obtained and the peak is spread over three accumulator cells. three maxima.

It is only intended here to illustrate the possible effects of the choice of quantization on the sensitivity of detection. The topic will be dealt with in detail in a later chapter. In addition, the interested reader might like to follow in more detail an excellent treatment of this topic given by Van Veen et al [Van Veen T. M. 1981] We shall press on now with some test images with which to check the transformation process.

61

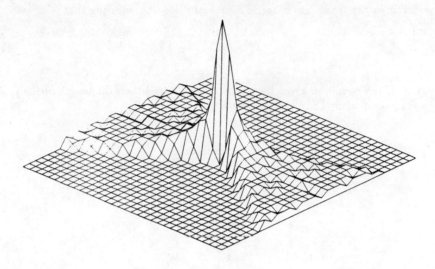

Fig 3.20 *Single maximum obtained for $\delta\theta \geq \tan^{-1}\left(\frac{\delta r}{L}\right)$*

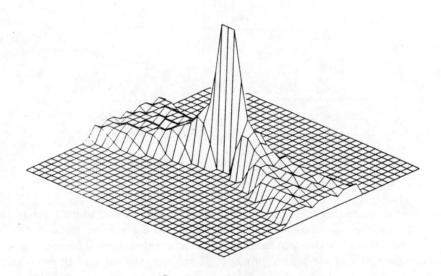

Fig 3.21 *Spread of values obtained for $\delta\theta < \tan^{-1}\left(\frac{\delta r}{L}\right)$*

3.8 Test Images

It is sometimes easier to debug a program if you have some idea of what the output should look like. This section provides some test images with which to check your program. These are shown in Fig. 3.22 . The size of the images is 128×128. The origin of the image is in the center of the picture. That is x and y are in the range $[-64, 63]$. The transform plane is also 128×128 with p in the range $[-64, 63]$ and θ in the range $[-2(\pi/128), \pi - 3(\pi/128)]$. The horizontal, $(p = 0.0, \theta = 90°)$, and the vertical, $(p = 0.0, \theta = 0°)$, lines should be used to test that the origins of both the image and the transform plane are as you expect them to be. The 45° line, $(p = 35, \theta = 45°)$, should tell you that p and θ are correctly quantised. When you have written and tested your program we will continue in the next chapter to consider how to treat the results of the transformation.

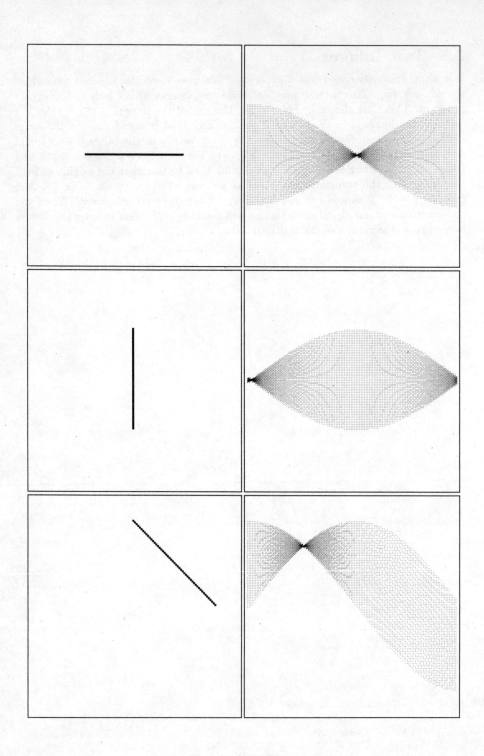

Fig 3.22 *Test Images*

CHAPTER 4

Postprocessing

In the previous chapter we have made our first sortie into the real world. We have learnt that real images need some careful preparation or preprocessing in order to extract suitable data for input to the transformation. We have dealt with programming a simple Hough algorithm and have thought a little about the quantisation in the transform space. Armed with the means to execute the transformation we are ready to press on with our task of shape detection.

The first obstacle we must overcome involves the extraction of information concerning shape from the transform plane. We will discover that the process of parametric transformation does not make explicit any information concerning connectivity and may breakdown when exposed to images containing correlated noise. This is the occurrence of perceptually meaningless features due to the accidental grouping of image points. These may appear where the noise levels are high or in the instance of multiple genuine features. They are not always obvious to the eye. It is a major disadvantage of the technique. Many methods deal with this problem. We will not complicate matters by reviewing them here but will develop a single method. This involves convolving the transform plane with a matched filter in order to extract the maxima associated with continuous straight line segments. A method for designing a suitable convolution filter is outlined. Permissible modifications which allow a computationally optimum implementation are also detailed. The reader, having followed through a detailed case study, will be in a much stronger position to consider alternative methods. These will be presented in chapter six.

The second obstacle we will tackle involves the treatment of discrete data. An attempt is made to bridge the gap between theory and application by interpreting available analytical work in terms of geometric propositions which are perhaps easier to follow for those without advanced mathematical training and which give the potential user a more practical understanding of the transformation process. Many aspects of the technique not immediately obvious in a purely analytical treatment become clear when expressed geometrically, and the need to evaluate complicated integrals is avoided.

4.1 Results of the transformation

What we find when we execute the transformation is that everything looks exactly as we expect it to look. For example, if we take the edge image corresponding to our wooden block and transform it, we see in Fig. 4.1 that there are twelve areas of maximum intensity. These correspond to the twelve visible edges of the block. They are grouped into four sets of parallel lines. That is, the maxima corresponding to a particular set of parallel lines are grouped according to the same value of θ. As we have said previously, the transform is uniquely defined by θ in the range $[0, \pi]$ and p in the range $[-p, p]$. Accordingly in the transform plane shown, this range of θ is chosen for the abscissa and the ordinate is in the range $[-I_D/2, (I_D/2) - 1)]$ where $I_D \times I_D$ are the dimensions of the image.

Up to now we have not given much thought to extracting the maxima from the transform space. We have assumed that thresholding would be sufficient. Again we are about to collide head-on with the real world where nothing is so simple. However, let's proceed cautiously with the simple approach and see what happens.

The first thing that we need is an appropriate threshold. If we take a closer look at our edge image of the wooden block, Fig. 4.2 , we see that most of the lines are made up of small vertical or horizontal segments. Even worse than this is that some lines which appear to the eye to be continuous are actually composed of more than one digital line. For example, see the lines indicated by arrows. The total length of this 'apparent' line is on the order of 60 or 80 pixels whereas the length of each contributing segment is approximately 20 pixels. It would therefore seem reasonable

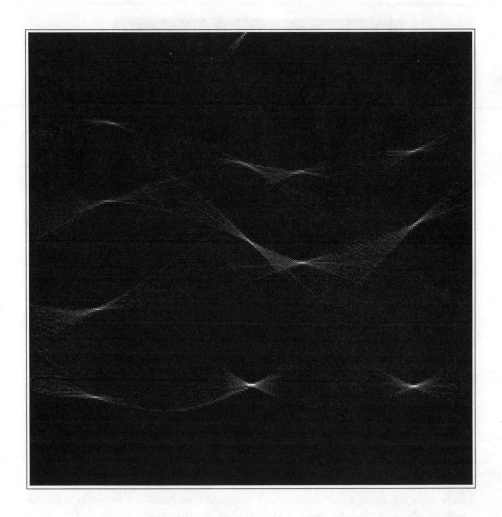

Fig 4.1 *Intensity map of transform plane*

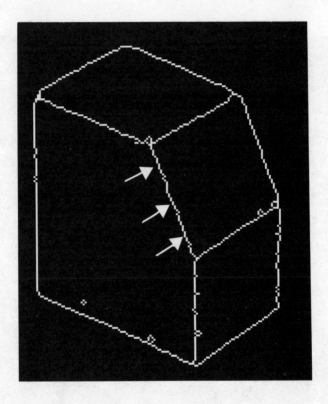

Fig 4.2 *Digital line splitting*

to set a correspondingly low threshold of 20 pixels to cope with this digital line splitting.

If we write a search for local maxima and threshold algorithm and we apply it to the transform plane of Fig. 4.1 with a threshold of 20, the result, shown in Fig. 4.3 , is not quite what we would expect! There are many spurious maxima not indicative of continuous straight lines in the image. What has happened is that we have come across a major disadvantage of the technique. The Hough transform provides no information concerning connectivity. The result is that correlated noise causes the process to detect perceptually meaningless co-linearities.

However, when we inspect the transform plane in Fig. 4.1 , we do not perceive all of the local maxima shown in Fig. 4.3 . What we see is a distinct distribution of intensity associated with each continuous straight line feature in image space.

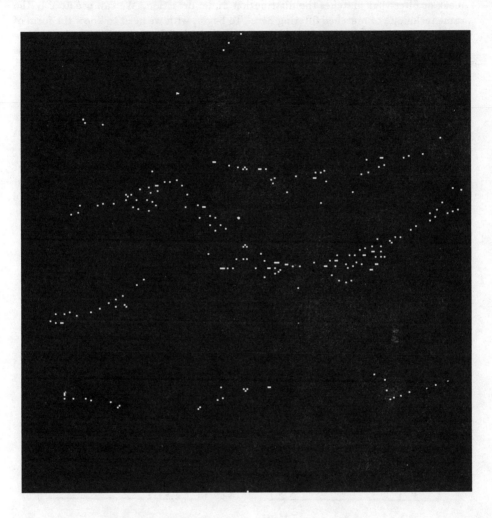

Fig 4.3 *Search for local maxima and threshold*

The distribution has the appearance of a butterfly with its wings extended in the θ direction. Should we therefore be looking for this particular distribution around a maximum value in transform space instead of simply trying to locate local maxima?

We have seen in chapter three that we can convolve an image with a function representing a notional form of the distribution we wish to detect. We do this by using a mask or filter that matches the distribution under detection. We can use exactly the same technique of matched filtering here. To begin, with we need to know the form of the distribution. The analytical form of the butterfly distribution in transform space has been deduced using a step by step geometric approach and a limiting process [Leavers et al 1987]:

$$H(p, \theta) = \frac{1}{|\sin(\theta - \alpha)|}$$

where the line under detection has a normal which subtends an angle α with the x axis. The complete derivation, taken from reference [Leavers et al 1987b], is given in appendix 1.

However, analytical expressions are not much use in the discrete world of digital images. Let's go on to see how we may bridge the gap between theory and application by deducing the form of a discrete convolution filter capable of locating the maxima associated with continuous straight lines.

4.2 The butterfly filter

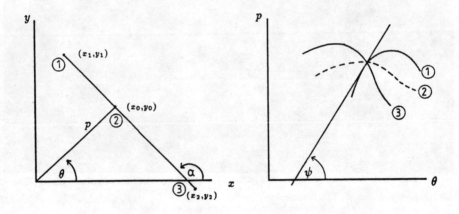

Fig 4.4 *Production of the boundary curves of Butterfly.*

The butterfly shape of the distribution surrounding the maxima in transform space can be modelled in the following way. Firstly, we reconsider what we have learnt about the desired properties of a convolution filter designed to locate particular distributions:

1. The form of the filter should mimic the distribution under detection such that a maximum, positive response is achieved when filter and desired distribution are co-incident.

2. When there is no change in the signal (in this case the intensity in a neighbourhood of the transform plane) then the result of operating with the filter should be a zero response. This property dictates that the elements of the filter should sum to zero.

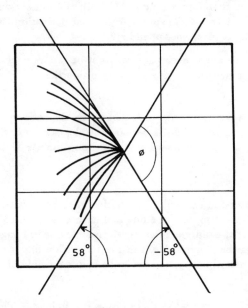

Fig 4.5 *Illustration of limits of displayed slope*

In Fig. 4.4 we see that the angle made by the tangent to a boundary curve at the points of intersection of the boundary curves is ψ. For a square image of side $2l$ and a given straight line segment, [Leavers et al 1987a]

$$-\sqrt{2}l \leq \tan\psi \leq \sqrt{2}l \tag{1}$$

For an $N \times N$ pixel image, having pixel dimension $(\Delta x)^2$, $l = \frac{1}{2}N\Delta x$. In the corresponding $N \times N$ transform image, having pixel dimension $\Delta p\Delta\theta$, the displayed slope, $\tan\chi$, is related to the true slope, $\tan\psi$, via

$$\tan\chi = \frac{\Delta\theta}{\Delta p}\tan\psi. \tag{2}$$

71

Hence the overall limits on the angles of the displayed wings are

$$-\sqrt{2}l\frac{\Delta\theta}{\Delta p} \leq \tan\chi \leq \sqrt{2}l\frac{\Delta\theta}{\Delta p} \tag{3}$$

But $\Delta\theta = \frac{\pi}{N}$ and $\Delta p = \sqrt{2}\Delta x$, therefore:

$$-\frac{\pi}{2} \leq \tan\chi \leq \frac{\pi}{2} \tag{4}$$

i.e.

$$-58° \leq \chi \leq 58° \tag{5}$$

The limiting angle is therefore a function of both the dimensions of the image and the quantisation of the transform space. A detailed derivation, taken from reference [Leavers et al 1987a], is given in Appendix 2.

The significance of the above derivation may not be immediately obvious. Attention paid to the general case gives us the following properties:

1. The angle ϕ between the wings of the butterfly depends upon the length of the line segment in image space. This is because the slopes of the wings of the butterfly are bounded by the location in image space of the endpoints of the line segment. See Fig. 4.4 .

2. The orientation of the butterfly distribution with respect to the horizontal axis depends both upon the length of the line and its position relative to the boundaries of the image space. For example, the longest possible line in image space corresponds to a diagonal across the screen. The transform of such a line is shown schematically in Fig. 4.5 . The butterfly shape is seen to be symmetric about the horizontal axis.

Let's consider in more detail what these properties indicate. The transformation of the end points of the line segment (labelled 1 and 3 in Fig. 4.4) generates the curves which form the boundaries of the wings of the butterfly as shown. Moving points 1 and 3 in Fig. 4.4   towards each other by equal amounts, i.e. shortening the line from both directions, is equivalent to closing up the wings of the butterfly (see Fig. 4.6). The curves may only move as shown from the limiting positions dictated by the maximum length of the line within image space.

If the line segment is shortened in both directions from its maximum length in image space, the change in the angle between the wings of the butterfly will not alter the symmetry of the distribution about the horizontal axis. Such symmetry *would* be destroyed if one were to consider, say, curve 2 remaining stationary and curve 1 moving (see Fig. 4.7). This would correspond to the shortening of a line segment from only one direction along the line and the butterfly shape is now no longer symmetric about the horizontal axis.

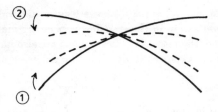

Fig 4.6 *Illustration of constraints on movement of boundaries.*

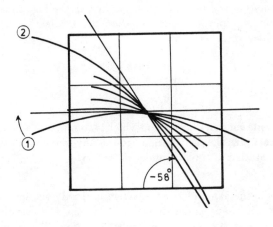

Fig 4.7 *Illustration of change in symmetry*
of butterfly shape.

Reference to Fig. 4.7 illustrates the fact that although the distribution now appears skewed, all contributing curves still pass through the central pixel and most, but not all, pass through the pixels to the right and left of centre.

The above information is important if we are to proceed with the design of the two dimensional convolution filter required to locate the maxima associated with continuous straight lines.

4.3 Designer Butterflies

We have already seen in chapter three that the length and width of the line in the edge image and the quantisation in the transform space are inextricably linked with respect to the spreading of the maxima. These effects are also important in the design of a digital filter. They are explored in detail in the following step by step design of a digital butterfly filter.

1. We have already noted that the application of large masks is computationally expensive so let's start by considering a 3×3 mask.

$$\begin{bmatrix} ? & ? & ? \\ ? & ? & ? \\ ? & ? & ? \end{bmatrix}$$

2. When the central pixel in a 3×3 convolution window is co-incident with a maximum value, then we have seen that the information along the outermost diagonal elements of the corresponding locations in transform space refers to the orientation of the butterfly with respect to the horizontal axis and is determined by the endpoints of the line. This information will be different according to the line under detection. It is therefore expedient to suppress the information which refers to the orientation of the butterfly. The filter then becomes

$$\begin{bmatrix} 0 & ? & 0 \\ ? & ? & ? \\ 0 & ? & 0 \end{bmatrix}$$

The remaining elements contain information which is common to all line segments and can be used to characterize the distribution around any maximum value irrespective of the length or orientation of the line under detection.

3. Remembering that the value of the transform is simply the length of the probe line coincident with the shape under detection, then the value of the central pixel will always equal the length, L, of the line under detection. The mask becomes:

$$\begin{bmatrix} 0 & ? & 0 \\ ? & L & ? \\ 0 & ? & 0 \end{bmatrix}$$

4. If the probe line is rotated about the origin by some angle $\delta\theta$ then we have seen that for the detection of digitized line segments by the location of a single maximum in the transform space:

$$\delta\theta > \tan^{-1}\left(\frac{\delta r}{L}\right)$$

If the above condition is true then the length of the probe line coincident with the image line is given by

$$l = \frac{\delta r}{\sin\delta\theta} \tag{6}$$

The filter now becomes

$$\begin{bmatrix} 0 & ? & 0 \\ l & L & l \\ 0 & ? & 0 \end{bmatrix}$$

5. If the lines under detection have a width of 1 pixel and p is quantized in integer steps then the values above and below a maximum value will be zero. This is because the probe line will not cut the image line at any point. To ensure that the elements of the mask sum to zero, factors of

$$-\frac{2l + L}{2}$$

are included at these locations where the distribution is expected to have a zero value. The inclusion of these elements therefore has no effect on the efficacy of the filter but ensures that the sum of the elements is zero. The completed filter now becomes

$$\begin{bmatrix} 0 & -\frac{2l+L}{2} & 0 \\ l & L & l \\ 0 & -\frac{2l+L}{2} & 0 \end{bmatrix} \tag{7}$$

4.4 Putting Things to Work

In this section we make the elements of the butterfly filter particular with respect to the example of straight line detection using our image of a wooden block. The dimension of the image under transformation in this case is 256×256. The transform accumulator is also a 256×256 array. The parameters p, θ are quantized in steps of $\delta\theta = \pi/256$ and $\delta p = 1$ respectively. Accordingly p and θ are in the ranges:

$$-128 \le p \le 128$$
$$-2\pi/256 \le \theta \le \pi - (3\pi/256)$$

If it is assumed that the maximum length of lines under detection will be of the order of 160 pixels for an image of this size, then the value of the central pixel, L, becomes 160. For the given values of δp and $\delta\theta$, l becomes 81. Hence a filter of the form

$$\begin{bmatrix} 0 & -2 & 0 \\ 1 & 2 & 1 \\ 0 & -2 & 0 \end{bmatrix} \tag{8}$$

75

will be appropriate to use in this particular case.

The filter suppresses the information concerning the orientation of the butterfly and treats the dense packing of the curves to the left and the right of the maximum value and the absence of curves from the top and the bottom central pixels as the only significant information.

The use of such a mask can greatly increase computational efficiency as the filter may be decomposed into two one-dimensional filters as follows. First a

$$\begin{bmatrix} -2 \\ 2 \\ -2 \end{bmatrix}$$

convolution is applied in the p direction which requires only five additions; this is then followed by a further two additions of the values on either side of the central pixel in the θ direction. Thus only seven additions are required for a 3×3 convolution compared to the nine multiplications and eight additions normally required for such a convolution.

The filter remains successfully selective, however skewed the butterfly distributions may appear until the configuration appears which would correspond to a short line which is near the edge of the image space. In general an image will not be composed of such lines.

When a line segment is composed of smaller line segments, as will invariably be the case in a digital representation, then the lines will produce overlapping butterfly distributions which will cause closely grouped maxima in transform space. See Fig. 4.8 .

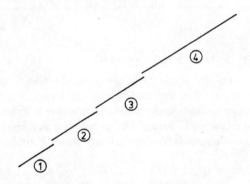

Fig 4.8 *Decomposition of digital line segment*

A small cluster of maxima in transform space will therefore characterize such line segments. It is possible to provide for this eventuality without greatly increasing the computational load by using an algorithm which finds the maximum value in an

$N \times M$ window in transform space and assigns to the central element of that window the value of the maximum. N and M may therefore be used as acceptable resolution criteria in p and θ without the need to sacrifice the ability to locate precisely the line segments in image space.

After application of the 3×3 convolution filter, a high response is checked to verify that the particular value is also a local maximum in an $N \times M$ window. In this way the resolution can be made realistically coarse whilst still allowing line segments to be precisely located in image space. For example, the line 4 in Fig. 4.8 will be the longest and most representative of the line segments 1, 2, 3 and 4 making up the longer line. A search in image space along a corridor of width $r \pm \Delta r$ would provide sufficient edge points to be representative of the entire line and to allow a fitting procedure to be applied to such a set of points. The end points may then be determined using search corridors generated by the fitted parameters.

Fig. 4.9 shows the transform accumulator after the application of the above operations. A threshold was applied such that only lines consisting of more than 20 pixels should be considered. Compare the result with that of simply locating local maxima and thresholding at 20.

4.5 Reconstruction

The technique may be assessed by considering how well the image may be reconstructed using the data extracted from the transformation. Such a reconstruction is illustrated and the various steps detailed. In addition to the lack of information concerning connectivity, a further disadvantage of the technique is that the end points of the lines are not made explicit by the transformation. We have to recover these using the parametric descriptions of the lines to search the edge image space.

In the first stage of the reconstruction, the transform parameters are used to aggregate the points of the edge image into lines by creating 'search-corridors' within the image space and hence partitioning the lines into sets corresponding to straight line segments.

Each corridor is created by taking a line:

$$y = p \operatorname{cosec}\theta - x \cot \theta$$

as the centre of a strip of width 5 pixels, i.e. ± 2 pixels which is twice the error in p. As edge points are encountered, they are deleted from the edge image and their co-ordinates stored. Should a search fail to find sufficient edge points, ($\geq 50\%$ of transform strength of that segment), the search corridor is rotated by an angle that represents the error in θ, ($\pm \pi/256$), the collected edge points are restored and the search is recommenced.

The line segments are treated in descending order of transform strength so that any spurious edge points due to the inclusion of vertex edge points will least affect the fitting process. The sets of edge points are passed to the fitting routine where the best straight line segment is fitted to each set of points. The algorithm involves using the transform parameter θ to rotate the points so that the estimated line is horizontal thus optimizing the fitting procedure. The least squares regression line is fitted and the adjusted transform parameters are returned. The complete algorithm is detailed

Fig 4.9 *Result of applying butterfly filter
with a threshold of 20*

in appendix 3. The end points of the lines are obtained using the optimized transform parameters.

Once all the line segments have been fitted and the end points of the line segments determined then the fitted lines are superimposed on the edge image. See Fig. 4.10 . The edge image has been altered to appear white on a mid-grey background. The fitted line segments (black) are shown superimposed on the edge image (shown in white).

4.6 Summary

Once again we seem to have arrived at a method of reconstruction! This is not what we want. The original plan was to recognize things using symbolic representations. Maybe this is a good moment to summarize what we've achieved and to consult the original plan. Our bottom up approach has certainly taken us a long way. In chapter two we have re-invented some pretty neat mathematics. In chapter three we have opened up the black boxes of edge detection and thinning and have reduced a whole mass of redundant information present in the raw image data to a primal sketch or edge map.

In this chapter we have developed a method of postprocessing the results of the transformation. Just as the real image contained a profusion of redundant information so the transform plane also contains much redundant information. This concerns not just perceptually meaningful groupings of image points but all possible groupings irrespective of contiguity. We have demonstrated that the application of a filter which exploits the characteristic butterfly shape of the maxima produced in transform space allows continuous straight line segments of any length and orientation to be detected. Spurious maxima created by discontinuous co-linearities in the image space are excluded even though the magnitude of such maxima may exceed that of true maxima which indicate shorter line segments. This fact is important because it allows a completely automatic detection process to be initiated irrespective of the length of the line segments, their orientation or the angles between intersecting lines, i.e. no previous knowledge of the image is required. Just as the end result of the preprocessing of the original image was a raw primal sketch so the result of our post-processing is a parametric primal sketch. Our achievements are illustrated in Fig. 4.11 . Data states are shown in Roman type and operations on the data are shown in italics.

What about our ultimate goal of symbolic representations? We haven't given this a thought so far. What the Hough transform does is to combine evidence concerning the grouping of low level feature points in an edge image. We are then able to use this information to extract features at a higher level. So far the only features we are able to extract are straight lines. Let's go on to consider curved features and then perhaps we can address the major question of the symbolic representation of shape.

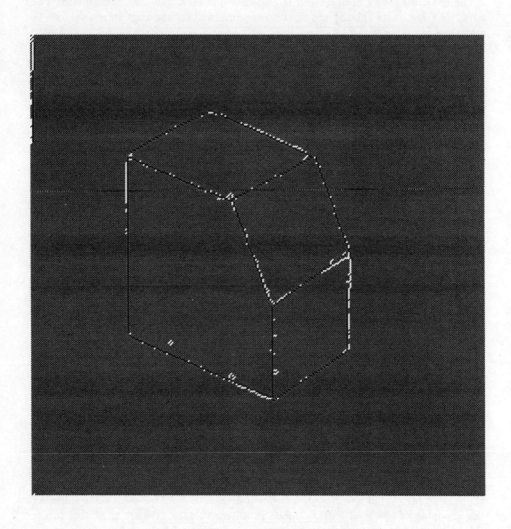

Fig 4.10 *Reconstruction superimposed
on original edge image*

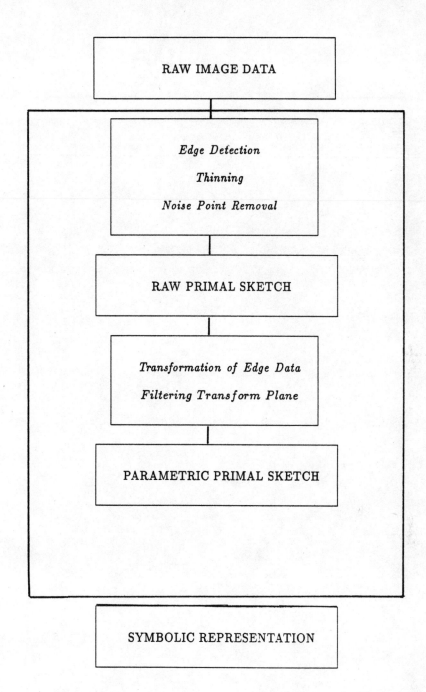

Fig 4.11 *Modular Shape Detection System*

CHAPTER 5

Representing Shape

In chapter one we decided that decomposition is an essential prerequisite for an efficient symbolic representation of shape. Accordingly we have pursued the Hough transform method with the aim of extracting the component features of shape from the image. We are so far able to decompose an image into straight lines. In this chapter we go on to consider the extraction of curved features such as arcs of circles or ellipses.

The theory behind straight line detection leads very naturally to the detection of other analytically defined shapes. Unfortunately, using this standard form of Hough transform becomes impractical when more than two parameters are under detection. This is because of increased storage and computational requirements. Solutions to these difficulties continue to generate a steady stream of additions to the literature. We will consider just one of them here. This alternative method uses the two dimensional straight line transformation iteratively in order to extract first straight line features and then circular arcs. We will use this method as it allows us to develop a representation of shape using those concepts we are already familiar with. Other methods will be reviewed in the next chapter.

We then go on to assess the Hough transform according to the remaining criteria for a good representation of shape. We see that it is indeed possible to build robust symbolic representations of shape using the Hough transform.

5.1 From Lines to Circles

In chapter two we saw that doing the maths offered abstract insights not immediately available in a purely intuitive treatment. If we review the maths again we will discover that it is not so conceptually difficult to progress from straight lines to circles and ellipses.

Essential to the method is the ability to define a δ-function whose argument evaluates to zero. To do this we generalize our defining equation:

$$H(p, \xi) = \iint\limits_{D} I(x, y) \delta \left(p - C(x, y; \xi) \right) dx \, dy \qquad (1)$$

where $I(x, y)$ is an arbitrary generalized function [Gelfand et al 1966] defined on the xy plane D and again represents our image. The argument of the δ- function defines some family of curves in the xy plane parametrized by the scalar p and the components $\xi_1, \xi_2, \ldots \xi_n$ of the vector ξ [Deans 1981]. That is, the argument of the delta function takes the form of the shape under detection.

If we progress to features other than straight lines the same basic methodology applies. Where $I(x, y)$ represents a binary image, the integral of equation (1) will have a value equal to the length of intersection of the image points and the curve defined by:

$$p = C(x, y; \xi) \qquad (2)$$

The argument of the delta function evaluates to zero at all values of (x, y) that are solutions to this equation To execute the transformation, for every point, (x_i, y_i), of the image, i is fixed and the values p_j are calculated using stepwise increments of the components of ξ. Each point in the transform space will refer to a possible curve in image space which passes through the point (x_i, y_i).

Things look a bit more complicated now so let's look at a particular example, the circle, and relate it to what we already know concerning straight line detection. The equation of a circle can be written as:

$$(x - x_0)^2 + (y - y_0)^2 = p^2 \qquad (3)$$

where x_0 and y_0 are the center co-ordinates of the circle and p is its radius. Whereas the straight line needed two parameters, (p, θ), to define it, the circle needs three, (p, x_0, y_0). This implies that we now need a three dimensional accumulator in which to store the results of the transformation.

In principle we can use this method to detect any curve which can be described analytically in the form $F(x, y) = 0$. In practice things soon become computationally unrealistic for three reasons:

1. **Memory requirements.** The determination of n parameters each resolved into T intervals requires an accumulator of T^n elements. For example an ellipse having five parameters, would require a five dimensional accumulator having T^5 elements.

2. **Computational Complexity.** As the number of parameters increases so too does the number of calculations. This scales exponentially with the dimensionality of the problem.

3. **Parameter Extraction.** Locating the maxima in transform space associated with the features under detection will involve searching an n dimensional accumulator.

The literature contains many methods aimed at solving these problems. We will consider just one of them here. Others will be reviewed in the next chapter.

5.2 Double Houghing

We can see that using the above extension of the standard Hough Transform to extract curved features requires that a new parametric transform space be used with respect to each feature under detection. The dimensionality of each transform space is a function of the number of parameters associated with a particular feature. An alternative theoretical approach [Leavers 1988a] deduces that the parametric information associated with curved features in image space may be encoded in a compact form using a second transformation.

We saw in chapter two that a curved shape in image space is uniquely represented, to some predetermined resolution, by the loci of the maxima generated in the transform space. Thus the shape may be reconstructed at each point by its tangents in the neighbourhood of those points, see [Leavers et al 1987b]. Let's consider how we may formalise and exploit this phenomena.

The standard Hough Transform for straight line detection is given by:

$$H(p, \xi) = \int_D I(\mathbf{x}) \delta \left(p - \xi \cdot \mathbf{x} \right) d\mathbf{x}$$

where $\xi = (\cos \theta, \sin \theta)$ and $\mathbf{x} = (x, y)$. We have seen that replacing the argument of the δ-function allows us to detect other shapes but that this is computationally impractical. A further alternative is to replace $I(\mathbf{x})$ with a curve having the form of a δ-function concentrated uniformly, with unit density with respect to arc length, on some analytically defined curve. The defining equation then becomes:

$$H(p, \xi) = \int\limits_{D} a(\mathbf{x}) \delta\left(r - C(\mathbf{x}; \psi)\right) \delta(p - \xi \cdot \mathbf{x}) d\mathbf{x} \tag{4}$$

The argument of this new δ-function defines some family of curves in the xy plane parametrized by the scalar r and the components $\psi_1, \psi_2, \ldots \psi_n$ of the vector ψ and $a(\mathbf{x})$ is a density function which ensures that the argument of the delta function has unit density at all points along the curve in accordance with the assumed property of uniform density.

It has been shown in reference [Leavers et al 1987b] that when the image undergoing transformation is a δ-function curve, then the maxima generated in transform space correspond to the tangents to that curve at the points where curve and tangent have a common normal and this is exactly the phenomena we observe. Let's see how we can put this to work with respect to extracting information concerning curved features.

If we transform the image of a circle centred on the origin, we obtain the intensity map of the transform plane shown in Fig. 5.1 . We see that the maxima associated with the tangents to the circle are located along two straight lines, each displaced from the origin in transform space by a distance a, the radius of the circle. We can locate these maxima using a filtering process similar to that employed to locate the maxima associated with the butterfly distribution, see reference [Leavers at al 1987a]. When we have done this, we are left with a binary image of two straight lines. We can then transform this image to produce two maxima in a second transform space. What we have done is to take the spatially extended data in the first transform plane and transform it into the compact form we have associated with straight line detection. We can then filter this second transform space, just as we have done for straight line features, only this time the position of the maxima will tell us the radius of the circle. Fig. 5.1 shows the image of a circle centred on the origin and the first and second transform planes obtained as described above.

Unfortunately all circles are not centred on the origin! What happens if we displace the circle? Each point (x, y) in the image space is now shifted to a new point $(x - x_0, y - y_0)$ where (x_0, y_0) are the new centre co-ordinates of the circle. This means that each maximum generated in the transform space is also shifted to:

$$p_{max} \mapsto (x - x_0) \cos \theta + (y - y_0) \sin \theta$$

which can be re-written for clarity as:

$$p_{max} \mapsto a - (x_0^2 + y_0^2)^{\frac{1}{2}} \cos\left(\theta - \tan^{-1}\left(\frac{y_0}{x_0}\right)\right) \tag{5}$$

This is the equation of a sinusoid with period, 2π, amplitude, $A = (x_0^2 + y_0^2)^{\frac{1}{2}}$ and phase $\phi = \tan^{-1}\left(\frac{y_0}{x_0}\right)$. The process is illustrated diagrammatically in Fig. 5.2 . We can see that although we have lost the straight lines associated with the circle centred on the origin there are still quite distinct linear segments. These may be

86

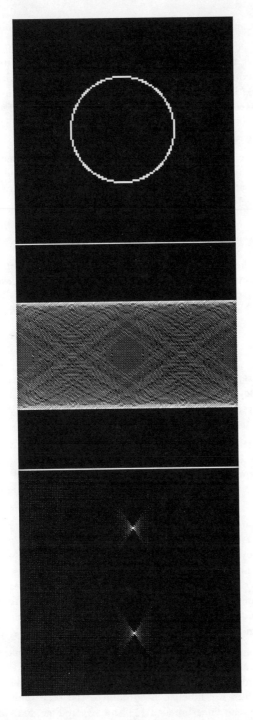

Fig 5.1 *Image of circle with first and second transform planes*

used as approximations to straight lines passing through the points of inflexion of the sinusoids.

In summary, the first transform plane is filtered to produce a binary representation of the loci of the maxima. This binary image is then used as the input to the second transformation. The linear portions of the sinusoids will produce maxima in this second transform space, the locus of which define the equations of the tangents to the sinusoids at the points of inflexion. In this way we can recover the three parameters which define the circle. See reference [Leavers 1988a].

It is therefore possible to parametrize circles using a twice iterated, two-dimensional transformation. This means that the methodology can be used to decompose a binary edge image into its constituent features where those features are of two basic types, straight lines and circles or arcs of circles.

5.3 Towards a Representation of Shape

In chapter one we looked at previous solutions to the problems of shape representation and from them compiled a list of criteria essential to a good representation of shape. Now that we are in a much better position to appreciate the details, let's review this list with respect to the Hough Transform and from this develop a system of symbolic representation of shape.

5.3.1 Decomposition

The power of any representation derives from an allowance of free combinations of components. A set of primitives or irreducible components should therefore be associated with the representation. Where the set of primitives is small, particularly fine discriminations need not be made in the detection process.

The methodology we have developed using the Hough Transform can be used to decompose a binary edge image into its constituent features or more properly we should call them shape primitives. The primitives which we shall use are of two basic types, straight lines and arcs of circles. A flow diagram of the algorithm is shown in Fig. 5.3 .

By way of illustration, image(1), shown in Fig. 5.4 is of an hexagonal nut. An intensity map of the transform plane of image(1) is shown in Fig. 5.5 . The transform is uniquely defined by θ in the range $[0, \pi]$ and p in the range $[-p, p]$. Accordingly, for the transform plane, this range of θ is chosen for the abscissa and the ordinate is in the range $[-I_D/2, (I_D/2) - 1)]$ where $I_D \times I_D$ are the dimensions of the image. All intensity maps of transform planes illustrated in this chapter are configured in this way. In addition, images and intensity maps of transform planes are shown here in reverse contrast in order to facilitate labelling.

Each of the six lines which form the outer boundary of the shape in image(1) are represented in the transform plane by a maximum value whose locus gives the (p, θ) parameters associated with the line in image space. The maxima in transform space are ringed in black and are labelled according to the corresponding lines in image space. For example, the lines labelled (1) and (2) in Fig. 5.4 each have normals through the origin of length p and those normals are at angles to the horizontal axis of 0 and $\pi/3$ respectively.

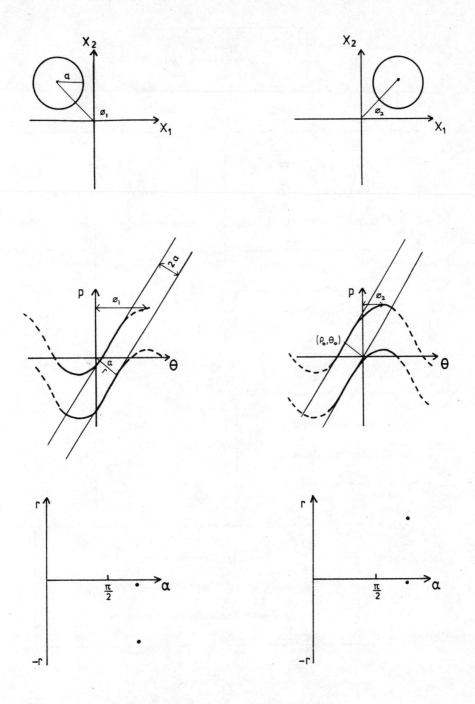

Fig 5.2 *Iterative Transformation of Circle*

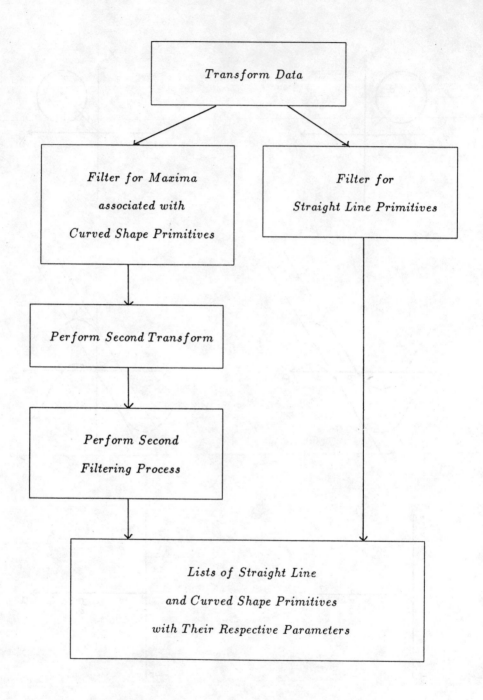

Fig 5.3 *Algorithm for Decomposition of Image*

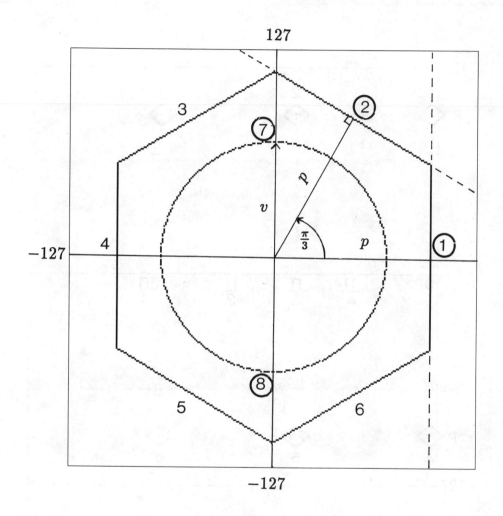

Fig 5.4 *Image(1) Hexagonal Nut*

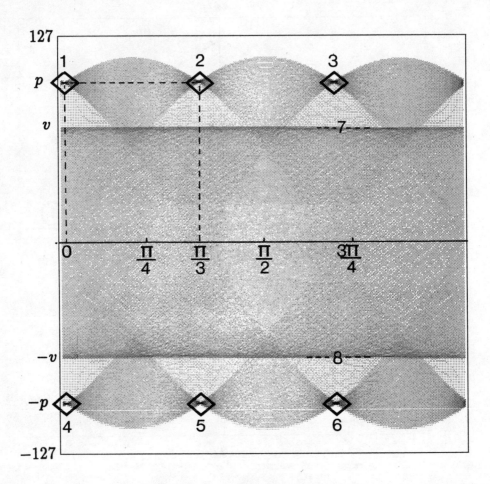

Fig 5.5 *First Transform Plane of Image(1)*

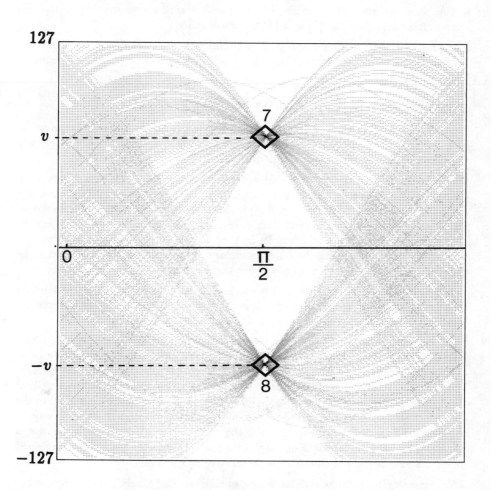

Fig 5.6 *Second Transform Plane of Image(1)*

93

The inner boundary of the shape shown in Fig. 5.4 is formed by a circle centred on the origin and of radius v. The maxima generated by this portion of the image are all located at a distance $\pm v$ from the origin in the transform space. These maxima correspond to the tangents to the circle. They are labelled (7) and (8) according to which semi-circular arc they correspond. The maxima may be located using an appropriate matched digital filter [Leavers et al 1987a]. This filtered image is then used as input to a second transformation. The resulting intensity map is shown in Fig. 5.6 and gives the location of two maxima each corresponding to the two semi-circular arcs, labelled (7) and (8), in image space.

The process therefore allows a digital edge image to be decomposed into its constituent shape primitives where those shape primitives are straight line segments or arcs of conic section.

5.3.2 Geometric and Spatial Relations

It is not sufficient to simply decompose the image into its constituent shape primitives. In addition, the representation should also make explicit the geometric and spatial relations between those shape primitives.

Once the transformation and filtering processes are complete, the parameters associated with the shape primitives are known. These parameters are labelled p and θ for the first transformation and v and λ for the second transformation. Inspection of the parameters will yield the geometric properties and relative spatial arrangements of the shape primitives. For example, in Fig. 5.4 the angle between each pair of connected lines constituting the outer boundary of the object is $2\pi/3$. This may be deduced by considering the angles between the normals to those pairs of lines.

Parallelism between pairs of straight lines may be deduced by inspection of the first transform plane and the grouping of the maxima having the same value of θ. Image(1) generates three sets of parallel lines, (1,4), (2,5) and (3,6), see Fig. 5.5 .

Knowledge of the relative lengths of the primitives may be obtained from the transformation in the following way. Each point on a straight line will contribute a value of 1 to the value of the maximum in transform space associated with that straight line. The value of the maximum may thus be used as a measure of the length of the line. Similarly for the curved shape primitives, the value of the maximum in the second transform space associated with a curved shape primitive in the image space will be a measure of the relative length of that curved shape primitive. In the case of image(1), Fig. 5.4 , all straight line segments are of equal length and this is reflected in the magnitude of intensities of the corresponding maxima.

The symmetry between particular shape primitives may be determined by examination of the transform parameters. Image(1), Fig. 5.4 , is bi-laterally symmetric about the origin in image space and this is reflected in the locus of the maxima in the transform space, Fig. 5.5 .

In the case of the curved shape primitives, the algebraic distance between respective centres of curvature is invariant under the operations of rotation and translation and may be deduced by consideration of the respective values of λ associated with those primitives. Thus, concentricity may be deduced in the second transform plane where curved shape primitives having the same value of λ will have concentric centers of curvature. This is illustrated by image(2) in Fig. 5.7 and its first and second

94

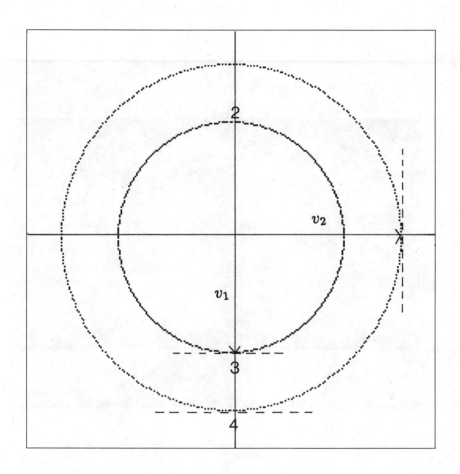

Fig 5.7 *Image(2) Circular Washer*

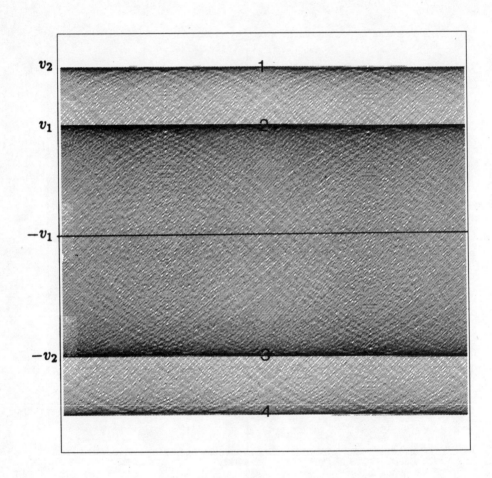

Fig 5.8 *First Transform Plane of Image(2)*

96

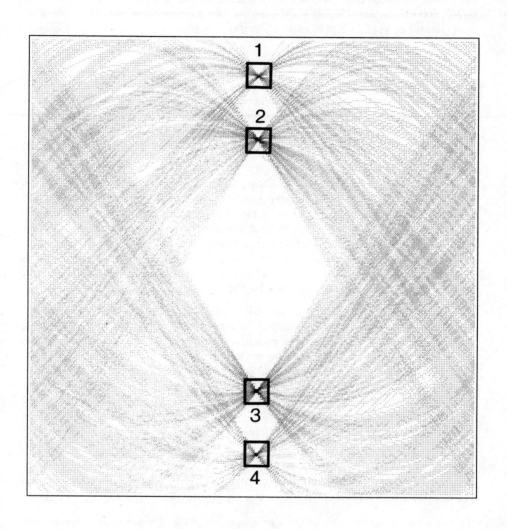

Fig 5.9 *Second Transform Plane of Image(2)*

transform planes, shown in Fig. 5.8 and Fig. 5.9 respectively. In the first transform plane, maxima corresponding to the tangents to the two concentric circles in image space are situated at distances of $\pm v_1$ and $\pm v_2$ from the origin where v_1 and v_2 are the radii of the concentric circles. This first transform plane is filtered to locate the maxima and the filtered image is transformed. Fig. 5.9 shows the result of this second transformation. Clearly visible are the four maxima corresponding to the four semi-circular arcs, (1), (2), (3) and (4), in image space.

5.3.3 Saliency

The representation should be such that gross or salient features associated with shape can be made explicit and used to bring essential information to the foreground allowing smaller and more easily manipulated descriptions to suffice. The ability to extract two or three salient primitive components means that objects can be quickly recognised even when they are partially occluded or their images are extensively degraded.

Salient features may be extracted by simply determining the pair or triplet of shape primitives having the greatest or near greatest values of maxima, m_i^j, in either the first or second transform plane. The method takes centrally positioned model images, transforms those images; filters the first and second transforms of the image for maxima and stores, as triplets of data, (p_i, θ_i, m_i^1) and (v_i, λ_i, m_i^2), the information associated with those maxima. The data triplets are ordered on the strength of the maxima. The topmost pair or triplet of data sets from these ordered lists become, where appropriate, the salient features for that particular object.

Knowing that each description of an object has a set of salient features does not help to distinguish one particular object from another. In the case of straight lines, the angle between the salient shape primitives is different in the case of each model image and, because angular differences are invariant under the operations of translation, rotation and scaling, the difference between images, having salient straight line configurations, may be expressed by these angular differences, $\Delta\theta_{ij}^{model}$. For angular differences $> \pi/2$ the value $\pi - \Delta\theta$ is stored. A similar constraint is applied to the values of $\Delta\theta$ extracted from the images. This is necessary when the transform plane is represented in the ranges $[0, \pi]$ and $[-p, p]$.

A similar process deals with the maxima in the second transform plane. In the case of circular arcs, the relative positions of respective centres of curvature are invariant under the operations of rotation and translation and this invariance is a function of the angular differences, $\Delta\lambda_{ij}$, between the maxima in the second transform space.

To give a particular example of the use of saliency to identify particular objects from a known set, image(1), Fig. 5.4 , has six straight line shape primitives associated with it. No pair or triplet of maxima may be chosen as its salient features as all six lines are of equal length. The set of six is therefore chosen to represent this image. By contrast, image(2), Fig. 5.7 , has no straight line shape primitives and consequently no isolated maxima in the first transform plane. However, it does have four maxima in the second transform plane. These maxima are located at the same value of λ thus inferring the concentric arrangement of circles characteristic of the washer in image space. The maxima correspond to the four semi-circular arcs, (1) to (4) that form the outer boundary of the washer in image(2).

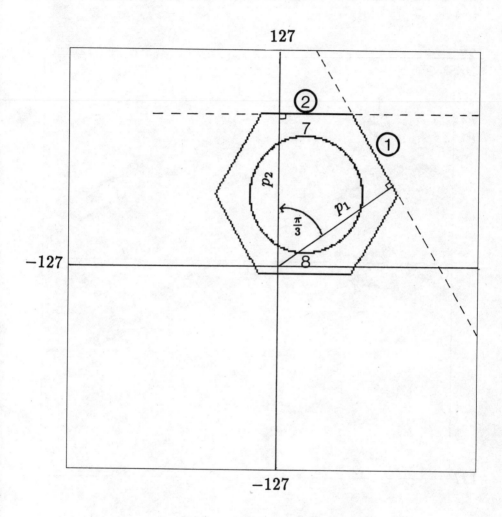

127

−127

−127

Fig 5.10 *Image(3) Hexagonal Nut Rotated and Shifted*

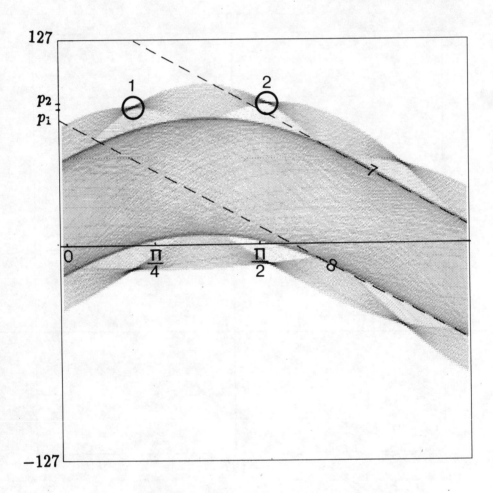

Fig 5.11 *First Transform Plane of Image(3)*

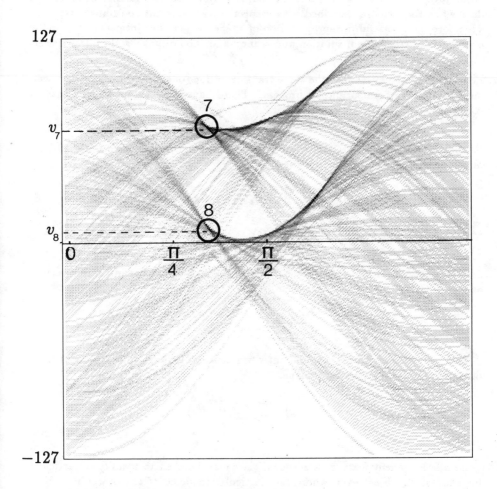

Fig 5.12 *Second Transform Plane of Image(3)*

101

5.3.4 Invariance

Information that is the basis of recognition should be invariant to the operations of translation, rotation and scaling.

It is a generally accepted principle that the symbolic description of an object will be represented in an object centred co-ordinate system but that the image input will be represented in a viewer centred co-ordinate system. This is a classic computer vision problem: matching an internal description of shape with an instance of image data when the two are described with respect to two different co-ordinate systems. Therefore, to be useful, a representation of shape should offer invariance under the operations of translation, rotation and scaling and should make explicit the viewer-object correspondence.

Let's consider the effect that the three transformations of shifting, rotation and scaling have on the transformation process. These have been discussed by Casasent [Casasent et al. 1987] and are as follows:

1. **Shifting** A shift, (a, b), in the image space corresponds to a displacement in the p direction only of the transform plane.

$$H(\theta, p) \overset{translation}{\longmapsto} H_t(\theta, p + t \cos(\theta - \alpha)) \tag{6}$$

where $t = (a^2 + b^2)^{\frac{1}{2}}$ and $\alpha = \tan^{-1}(b/a)$.

2. **Rotation** A rotation by an angle ϕ will cause a displacement in the θ direction only.

$$H(\theta, p) \overset{rotation}{\longmapsto} H_r(\theta + \phi, p) \tag{7}$$

3. **Scale** An image scaled by an amount s will cause a corresponding scaling in the p direction only of the transform plane.

$$H(\theta, p) \overset{scaling}{\longmapsto} H_s(\theta, p/s) \tag{8}$$

Once all the salient features are known they may be used to identify a particular instance of an object even where the particular instance of the object may be a rotated, shifted or scaled version of the model instance. Fig. 5.10 and Fig. 5.13 show the rotated, shifted and scaled images of the hexagonal nut and the circular washer. From their respective transform planes, it is possible to identify each object. Fig. 5.11 clearly shows that the maxima associated with the straight line primitives still reflect the angles between the lines in image space and this may be used to identify the hexagonal nut. The first transform plane, Fig. 5.14 , corresponding to the circular washer shown in Fig. 5.13 shows no maxima corresponding to straight line primitives. The second transform plane, Fig. 5.15 , clearly shows four maxima located at the same value of λ and this may be used to identify the circular washer.

102

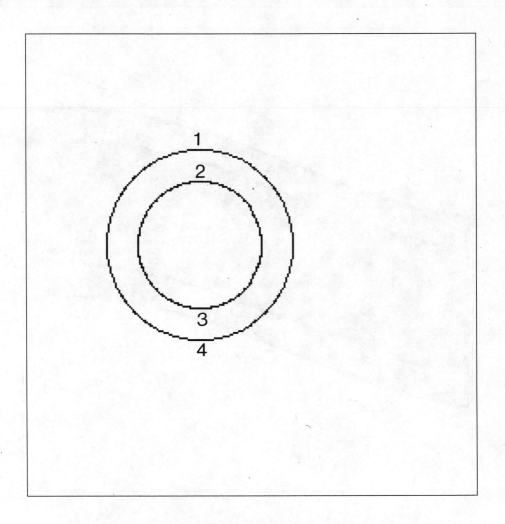

Fig 5.13 *Image(4) Circular Washer Shifted*

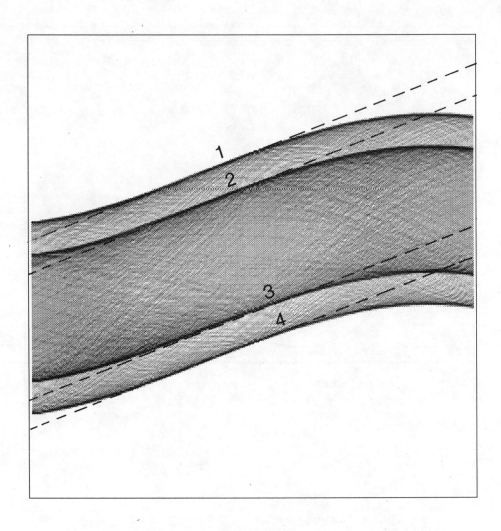

Fig 5.14 *First Transform Plane of Image(4)*

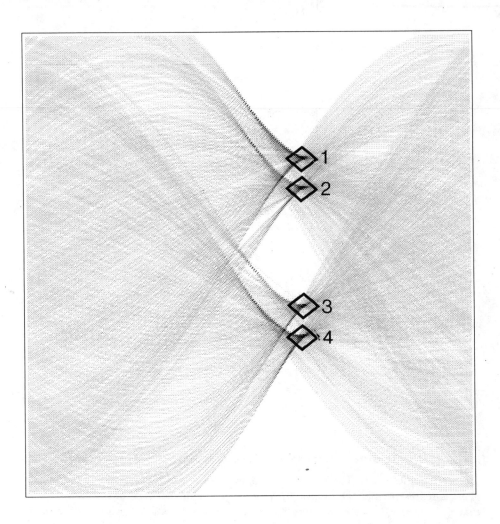

Fig 5.15 *Second Transform Plane of Image(4)*

Salient Features		
	θ	p
Model	θ_1	p_1
	θ_2	p_2
Image	ψ_1	r_1
	ψ_2	r_2

Fig 5.16 *Labelling of parameters associated with salient features*

The angle of rotation between the viewer centred co-ordinate system and the model centred co-ordinate system may be deduced using the parameters associated with the two sets of salient straight line shape primitives, model and image, labelled as shown in Fig. 5.16 . It is not possible to relate these parameters directly by inspection. Before the angle of rotation, ϕ, may be recovered four possibilities must be considered:

$$\phi_1 = (\pi + \theta_1) - \psi_1$$
$$\phi_2 = (\pi + \theta_2) - \psi_1$$
$$\phi_3 = (\pi + \theta_1) - \psi_2$$
$$\phi_4 = (\pi + \theta_2) - \psi_2$$

If $\phi_i = \phi_j$ then the corresponding values of θ_l and ψ_k may be used to pair the features.

Two ambiguities exist. The first is an ambiguity of π which occurs if the transform plane is represented in the ranges $[0, \pi]$ and $[-p, p]$ and the angle of rotation is such that ψ_2, ($\psi_1 < \psi_2$), passes through $\theta = \pi$ and reappears at $\theta > 0$ with the sign of p reversed. If no two values of ϕ_i and ϕ_j are equal then $\text{Min}(\phi_n) + \pi$ is applied and the correspondence sought.

A further π ambiguity occurs if the angle of rotation $> \pi$. This is resolved by checking if $\text{Max}(\phi_n) > \phi_i$, where ϕ_i is the angular parameter describing one of the pair of corresponding salient features. In this case $\phi_i \mapsto \phi_i + \pi$ and this is the angle of rotation.

Determination of the angle of rotation allows particular shape primitives in the edge image to be paired with their corresponding primitives in the computer model of the object. Once this is done, the shift and scaling parameters are calculated using the following system of equations:

$$\begin{pmatrix} r_1 & \cos(\theta_1 + \phi) & \sin(\theta_1 + \phi) \\ r_2 & \cos(\theta_2 + \phi) & \sin(\theta_2 + \phi) \\ r_3 & \cos(\theta_3 + \phi) & \sin(\theta_3 + \phi) \end{pmatrix} \begin{pmatrix} s \\ -x_0 \\ -y_0 \end{pmatrix} = \begin{pmatrix} p_1 \\ p_2 \\ p_3 \end{pmatrix}$$

where the (θ_i, p_i) are the parameters associated with the model shape primitives and the r_i are the parameters associated with the corresponding image shape primitives, ϕ is the angle of rotation, (x_0, y_0) are the shift parameters and s is the scaling factor.

5.3.5 Stability

It is important, at the low levels of computation, to ensure that access to the representation of an object does not depend on absolute judgements of quantitative detail.

With respect to the Hough transform technique, the existing work is such that the robustness of the technique in the presence of noise and extraneous or incomplete data is well tested and the efficacy of the method proven. We shall consider these methods in the next chapter. Here we will simply demonstrate qualitatively the robustness of the method in the presence of noise and occlusion.

Image(5), Fig. 5.17, shows a composition of three shapes, two of which suffer some degree of occlusion. In addition, random Gaussian noise with a zero mean and variance, σ_n, was added to each pixel in the test image. The resulting image was then rebinarized by thresholding at 0.5. A value of $\sigma = 0.25$ was chosen. The example is artificial and it should be understood that it is not possible to formulate any simple expression for the analysis of the effect of noise where such an expression would relate the noise present in the original image and the effect of that noise on the transformation. This occurs because any noise points present in the original image will, in the process of edge detection, be considered with respect to the neighbouring pixels. If the value of the function describing this relationship between neighbouring pixels is above some predetermined threshold then the noise point will be accepted as a candidate feature point or it will be disregarded. Thus, the edge detection stage of the preprocessing will alter, in a non-uniform way, the noise content of the original image.

The effect of transforming image(5), Fig. 5.17, is shown in Fig. 5.18. The transformation of random Gaussian noise results in the addition of background noise to the transform plane. The maxima associated with the straight lines in image space are ringed in black according to which line in image space they correspond. The maxima were located using a matched filter [Leavers et al 1987a]. The maxima associated with the curved shape primitives were also located using the appropriate matched filter [Leavers et al 1987a] and the resulting filtered image transformed. The result is shown Fig. 5.19. The maxima associated with the curved shape primitives are marked and numbered according to which arc of circle they correspond. These maxima were also located using a matched filter.

It is therefore possible, using the present technique, to demonstrate the recognition and location of objects even when there may be multiple objects present in the image

107

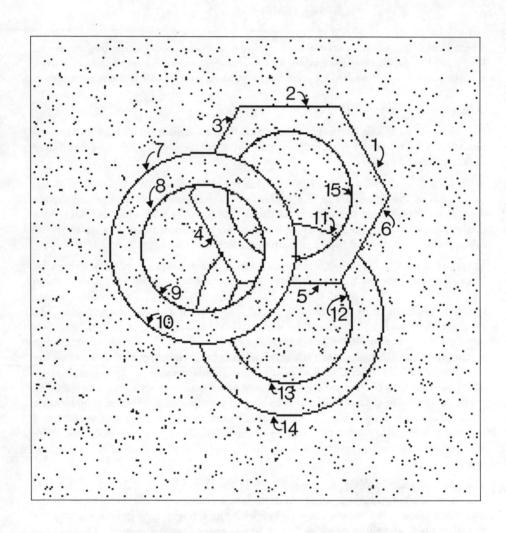

Fig 5.17 *Noisy Image(5) Showing Occluded Objects*

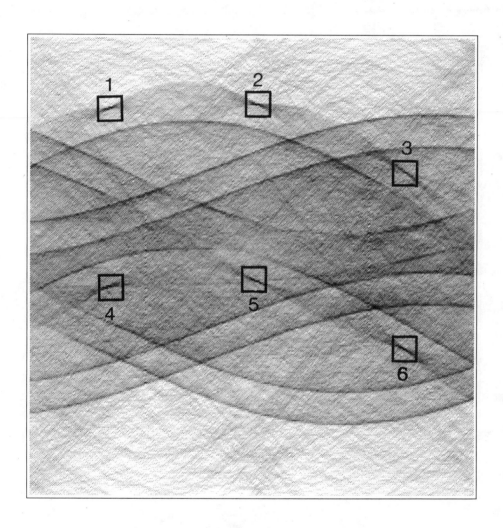

Fig 5.18 *First Transform Plane of Image(5)*

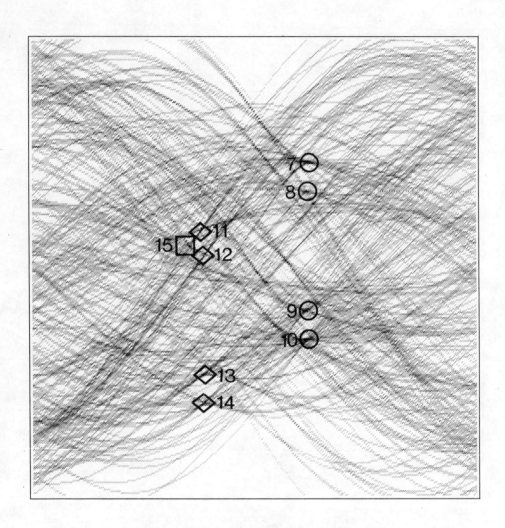

Fig 5.19 *Second Transform Plane of Image(5)*

and the object under detection is occluded or its image degraded. It should be noted however that the implementation and testing of a new method of shape detection is a major developmental task and each implementation will inevitably remain application dependent.

5.3.6 Accessibility

It is necessary to demonstrate that any proposed representation of shape is computationally realistic.

The development of fast, efficient implementations of parametric transformation methods has received much attention in the recent literature. Thus the question of computational accessibility is adequately addressed. The results of those studies will be reviewed in the next chapter.

5.4 Summary

We have demonstrated that the Hough transform can be used to decompose a binary edge image into its constituent shape primitives where those shape primitives are straight lines and arcs of circles. The technique makes explicit certain geometric properties and spatial relations between the shape primitives which are then used to code a representation of shape. Properties not made explicit by the representation are sequence of connectivity and regions. These are important concepts in the human perception and understanding of shape. Their absence in the present context will be discussed in the next chapter and possible solutions suggested. In addition we will see that our preferred method is not the only way of using the Hough transform as a method of shape detection. We will review in detail an alternative method.

CHAPTER 6

Which Hough?

In the preceeding chapters we have begun to learn something about the Hough Transform. If we wish to become more expert it is necessary to consult the available literature. An excellent comprehensive review of available methods up to and including 1987 is given by Illingworth [Illingworth et al 1988]. From such a review we can see that there are many different kinds of Hough Transform. It is difficult to know how to begin to categorize them. In this chapter we will develop a system of classification and update existing reviews where appropriate.

We start with the background to the technique and a brief historical review. Included are the standard references which no serious *Hougher* should be without. They form the backbone of any future study.

We have developed a method of shape detection which uses the Hough Transform to decompose an edge image into its constituent shape primitives. We then use the parameters associated with those primitives to build a symbolic representation of the shape under detection. This is not the only way of using the Hough Transform for shape detection. An alternative approach exists which treats the shape of an object in its entirety. We look at two such methods and review the more recent one in some detail.

The Hough Transform method of shape detection offers a unique potential concerning the automation of visual inspection tasks. However, in order to implement such systems successfully we need to be able to quantify performance aspects of the transformation process. This leads us to consider various additions to the basic theory aimed at formalizing the analysis of performance.

It is clear that any implementation of the method should run in a time commensurate with the needs of the application. Since the early 1970's various generations of *Houghers* have added steadily to the literature concerning optimization of the computation. We continue by categorizing the methods which seek to reduce the computational complexity and storage requirements of the standard technique. Optimization of the computation splits into three naturally occurring fundamentally different classifications. They are:

1. **Software Solutions.** These range from simply rewriting the basic algorithm in a computer-friendly form to a complete recasting of the transformation process.

2. **Parallel Processing.** Implementations that exploit general purpose parallel computer architectures.

3. **Dedicated Hardware.** Task specific computer architectures or VLSI designs.

Of the three categories, software solutions form the most significant contribution to the research as they are portable and do not require specific hardware. The advent of cheap accessible general purpose parallel systems has seen a steady increase in new parallel implementations of the Hough Transform. These systems are categorized according to the manner in which operations are executed in parallel, that is whether they function in the 'Single Instruction Multiple Data' (SIMD) mode or 'Multiple Instruction Multiple Data' (MIMD) mode. Task specific systems are mentioned for completeness. They are not reviewed.

A new family of Hough technique has appeared in the recent literature, the Probabilistic Houghs [Leavers 1991]. They are unique in that they can be generalized to deal with the detection of n parameters. These techniques offer many insights into the technique not previously available. They are treated in some detail as they are the latest innovation in 'Houghing' and are not reviewed, as yet, elsewhere.

6.1 Background

6.1.1 Historical

The Hough transform as such was first introduced by Paul Hough in 1962 [Hough 1962]. It was developed in connection with the study of particle tracks through the viewing field of a bubble chamber. It was one of the first attempts to automate a visual inspection task previously requiring hundreds of man-hours to execute.

Hough used the slope-intercept parametric representation of a line which led to the practical difficulty of an unbounded parameter space. Duda and Hart [Duda et al 1972] suggested that straight lines might be more usefully parametrized by the length, p, and the orientation, θ, of the normal vector to the line from the image origin.

However, parametric transformation was alive and well long before the birth of the Hough Transform. It was Deans [Deans 1981] who pointed out that the Hough transform is simply a special case of the Radon transform. Radon's classic paper [Radon 1917] in which the concept was first introduced had far-reaching influences in many branches of science.

Although Radon's work was not appreciated in the applied areas of science until the early 1960's, a tremendous amount of theoretical work was undertaken by the mathematicians, most notably Gel'fand, Graev and Vilenkin [Gel'fand et al 1966]. Deans was later instrumental in making much of this theoretical work accessible and comprehensible to scientists and engineers who lack advanced mathematical training. Use of the Radon transform has been widely exploited in the field of computerized tomography. This topic is extensively covered in the book, 'Applications of the Radon Transform', [Deans 1983].

Deans's paper, 'The Hough transform from the Radon transform' [Deans 1981], has become a standard reference in the field. In it, he develops the theory in three separate stages. The first follows the work of Gel'fand [Gel'fand et al 1966] in deducing analytically the transformation over a line segment.

In the second stage, Deans switches from this wholly analytical approach to an essentially geometric treatment. He points out that the value of the transform is simply the length of the line contained within $I(\mathbf{x})$, the function representing the image, and uses this fact to deduce expressions for the value of the transform over the unit pixel.

In the final stage, Deans suggests the manner in which the Radon/Hough transform may be generalized to detect analytically defined curves. This is done by rewriting the argument of the δ-function in the form of the curve under detection. We have looked at this in detail in the previous chapter and have called it the Standard Hough Transform (SHT).

Even before Deans formalized the method, various authors, for example [Kimme et al 1975] and [Weschler et al 1977], had used it to detect shapes other than straight lines. As we have already discovered, in the standard formulation, a major drawback of the method is an exponential growth of memory space requirement and computational cost as a function of the number of parameters under detection. Many solutions exist concerning these problems and we will investigate them later in the chapter.

6.1.2 Whole Shape Detection

A class of Hough techniques exist which do not decompose the image into its component features, for example, straight lines, but rather extract the shape in its entirety.
These methods do not offer explicitly the facility of decomposition required by our
formulation of a good representation of shape. They are however very useful in
certain applications and are included here for completeness.

A standard reference concerning such a formulation is Ballard [Ballard 1981]. He
has developed a Hough-like method to deal with shapes which cannot be represented
analytically. It is called the Generalized Hough Transform (GHT). We saw in chapter three that the edge detection stage of the preprocessing requires us to compute
the edge direction associated with each feature point. Ballard uses this directional
information in the following way in order to detect whole shapes. Each boundary
point in edge image space is stored as a vector relative to some reference point, that
is, the distance, r, and the direction, θ, of the line connecting the boundary point and
the reference point. Entries in a list are indexed by the local edge direction at the
boundary point. Such a list is called an R-table. Where shapes are of fixed orientation and scale, the R-table remains a two-dimensional accumulator array. To search
for shapes of arbitrary orientation and scale requires a further two parameters to be
added to the description of the shape. In this way Ballard reduces the maximum
dimensionality of the parameter space to four.

Ballard goes on to show how complex shapes can be decomposed into simpler shapes
and that it is possible to have a shape representation which can accommodate this
type of structural description. He does not develop this idea in any formal way. The
weakness of previous template-driven shape coding strategies is repeated in that a
particular shape can only be efficiently detected if one knows the transformation from
a canonical form of the shape to the instance of that shape. If the transformation is
not known then all plausible transformations must be tried.

For the interested reader, Davies has produced much work concerning both the theory
and implementation of the Generalized Hough Transform and this is summarized in
his book 'Machine Vision' [Davies 1990]. It is well worth reading. He is able to show
that the method works well in many industrial applications.

One of the more recent novel uses of the Hough Transform, which concerns whole
shape detection as opposed to feature segmentation, has been that of Casasent. The
approach differs strikingly from that advocated using our criteria for a good representation of shape. In their paper *Hough space transformations for discrimination
and distortion estimation* [Krishnapuram et al 1987], David Casasent and Raghuram
Krishnapuram present a technique which uses the Hough Transform to determine
multiple distortion parameters. Such parameters refer to scale, translation and rotation. The concept of shape is not made explicit in their work but their claim of
multi-class object discrimination may be interpreted to mean that different complex
shapes may be identified irrespective of the variations in the image due to scaling,
shifting or rotation.

The method approximates an object by a set of straight line segments which generate
a given two-dimensional pattern in Hough space. The normal (p, θ) parametrization
of the straight line is used. It is maintained that detecting peaks in the transform
space is difficult and unreliable especially where bias and noise are present. Thus no

116

effort is made to extract parametric information from the transform plane but rather matching is performed directly in the transform space.

If the object is scaled, rotated or translated, the pattern in Hough space will be a distorted version of the original reference pattern. Casasent and Krishnapuram apply transformations in the Hough space by shifting the accumulator bins in a prescribed way. This removes the distortions and recovers the viewer-object correspondence thus reconstructing the Hough Transform of the object in the original reference orientation. When this is done, a simple template matching with the Hough Transforms of different objects allows the object to be recognised.

In their paper they propose a simple three-level hierarchical matching-search procedure, the *Reduced Distortion Parameter Search* method. A set of results is presented which use computer generated two-dimensional aircraft imagery as the input data. They assume that the scale of the object under detection can be estimated using target range data and that the object is approximately centred using moments. A further assumption is that top-down only views of aircraft will allow the parallel lines of the fuselage to be used as estimators of the angle of rotation.

In the first level of the search, the translation is ignored and the Hough transform of the input object is matched with all allowed rotated versions of the Hough transform for each reference object. This is achieved by feeding the Hough transform of the input image and the reference image to a one dimensional correlator. This is possible because a rotation, as previously discussed, gives rise to a corresponding one dimensional shift along the θ axis in the Hough domain. The angle of rotation, ϕ is quantized in intervals of $\Delta\phi = 45°$. The rotation angle, ϕ_1, corresponding to the best match and its nearest neighbours, ϕ_2 and ϕ_3, are retained as the three most probable ϕ values.

From the centring accuracy given by the use of the first order moments, a maximum value of the shift parameter, t, is known. In this way, in the second level the value of t is assumed but it is still necessary to search the transform of the reference objects for all three expected values of the second shift parameter α for each of the three ϕ estimates obtained from the previous level. This can be easily achieved by applying only the α-distortion transforms to the Hough transforms of the reference objects. The quantisation steps for α are $\Delta\alpha = \pi/4$. A different α value results in a new Hough transform that is not simply a one dimensional shifted version of the original Hough transform. Thus this matching in the Hough space can be done by multiplying the corresponding elements of the Hough transforms and adding the products. This amounts to evaluating the correlation value at the centre point. These correlations, evaluated at one point, are referred to as projections. The ϕ value and three α values corresponding to the best match, α_1, and its two nearest neighbours, α_2 and α_3, are passed to level three.

In level three, a search is conducted from 0 to t_{max} for the three α values and the best ϕ value determined from level two. The quantisation steps for t are $\Delta t = 10$. The Hough transform for a new t value is once again a new Hough transform and this search, in increments of Δt, is performed in a similar manner to the search for α in level two. The number of t values and the range of t to be searched are set by the expected accuracy of the centring method. The best match yields the final values of t, α and ϕ and the object class estimates.

117

It is clear that this method, in order to function efficiently, requires the support of both contextual information and support from other methods of shape detection (use of first order moments). In addition, the method is computationally intensive. We will not consider further any technique of whole object detection as they lack the fundamental property of decomposition necessary for a good representation of shape.

6.2 Refinements

In this section we include work concerning the Hough Transform which deals with the nature of the transformation process and its performance as opposed to attempting to optimize the computation. It may be that a new theoretical framework for analysing the Hough Transform allows the use of powerful mathematical tools not otherwise available.

In its standard form, the transformation process cannot be considered in isolation. It requires extensive preprocessing of the raw image data to provide the correct input data. Postprocessing of the transform plane in the form of peak detection is often also required. The potential for error propagation is thus distributed across these various stages. We shall look at the theory with these categories in mind.

6.2.1 Preprocessing Considerations

The effects of noise and extraneous or incomplete data on the results of the transformation are a matter of concern when dealing with real image data. Two types of noise exist. The first occurs randomly and can be characterized by either random Gaussian, Laplacian or uniform noise. Such noise may be due to random corruption of the signal during the data acquisition process or it may be a normally distributed random error in the localization of image points due to the effects of digitizing continuous data. It is the kind of noise everyone likes to play with as it can be modelled mathematically and is easy to simulate. The characterization and prediction of the effects of such noise can be incorporated into any treatment of the accuracy of the results. The topic has been studied extensively. For example see [Shapiro 1975], [Iannino et al 1978], [Shapiro 1978] and [Shapiro et al 1979]. More recently [Risse 1989] and [Grimson et al 1990] have added to the body of knowledge concerning the effects of localization errors and noise on the performance of the transform.

Stephens [Stephens 1990] points out the strong relationship between the Maximum Likelihood Method and the Hough Transform. He defines a mathematically 'correct' form of the Hough Transform as the log of the Probability Density Function (PDF) of the output parameters. The PDF is a weighted sum of a uniform distribution and a normal distribution. Where multiple features are under detection, the combined PDF is formed by taking the product of the PDF's for each individual feature. The PDF also represents the error characteristics of the feature measurement. Stephens illustrates the method explicitly using an example of straight line detection and derives a model for the error characteristics using the normal parametrisation. The method has the advantage of being independent of image size and arrangement of accumulator cells. It deals with mathematically defined functions and can therefore call into use any of the standard techniques for locating maxima.

This particular formulation of the Hough transform [Stephens 1990] has a further advantage concerning performance. Conventional Hough Transforms have a sharp cut-off between a cell receiving a vote or not. This effect is analogous to aliasing distortion and has been studied by [Kiryati et al 1991a]. The smooth Gaussian roll-off of the PDF means that it has a lower bandwidth and generates less noise. However, it is pointed out that the calculation of this particular algorithm is much more computationally expensive than an SHT because for each image point as a substantial floating point expression has to be evaluated at each point in Hough space. However, Stephens suggests that in situations where there are many unknown parameters, conventional methods do not perform well and this particular technique may provide an effective alternative.

More problematic then the effects of random noise are those of a second type of noise, correlated noise. Peaks in the transform space correspond to instances of the feature under detection in the image. Brown [Brown 1983] has shown that where the image contains multiple features then the resulting transform space is a composition of the distributions associated with each single feature instance. Overlapping distributions add and the effect may be to distort the heights of peaks. In addition, false peaks may result giving rise to perceptually meaningless instances of shape in the image. This is the effect of correlated noise. More recently, Grimson et al [Grimson et al 1990] have published work which provides bounds on the likelihood of false peaks in the parameter space, as a function of noise, occlusion and tessellation effects. They point out that where complex recognition tasks are to be implemented, the probability of false peaks can be very high.

Attempts to deal with the effects of correlated noise by preferential segmentation of the image with respect to the shape under detection are given by Califano et al [Califano et al 1989] and Leavers [Leavers 1990a]. These two methods are reviewed in more detail at the end of this chapter.

Another method which seeks to alleviate the effects of correlated noise is that of Yuen [Yuen 1991]. It is called the Connective Hough Transform (CHT). The method is concerned with straight line detection but the author states that the idea can be generalized to deal with other parametric curves. The implementation uses the Dynamic Combinatorial Hough Transform (DCHT) [Leavers et al 1989] method of calculation and accumulation. Using the CHT method, all feature points, as they are detected, are tested for connectivity with respect to neighbouring points. In this way the CHT is a principled method of curve tracing as attention is focused concerning connectivity. In the case of straight line detection the method has been shown to work on real image data containing a profusion of correlated noise. See reference [Yuen 1991].

6.2.2 Postprocessing Considerations

Evaluation of the information generated in the transform space may present difficulties. In the particular case of circle detection, Gerig [Gerig et al 1986] links image and accumulator spaces in a way that allows for a more accurate extraction of the parameters in the case of circle detection. He uses a technique which maps information from the parameter space back to the image space. After the execution of a first transformation, information from the parameter space is used to assign to each image point a most probable parametrisation. A second transformation is performed where, for each image point, only the cell in parameter space associated with the most probable parametrisation of that image point is incremented. The technique works well in that it is a reliable strategy for interpreting the accumulator space. It is however still computationally complex and offers no reduction in memory allocation.

As we have seen in chapter four, problems associated with the detection of maxima in the transform space may be partially solved by the use of matched filtering techniques to detect those maxima [Leavers et al 1987a]. In order to design such filters, it is necessary to incorporate knowledge of the dimensions of the features under detection and the quantisation of both the image and the transform space. We have seen in chapter four that, at any scale of discretization of the accumulator array, a high count in a particular cell may be the combined effect of several insignificant peaks rather than a single significant one. Moreover, a true peak may be split between several accumulator cells and not detected. In reference [Meerveen et al 1988], the problems are illustrated by the application of the Hough Transform to detect straight lines in an image containing 'multiscale curves'. At any fixed resolution false maxima and peak spreading are apparent. In the case of straight line detection, peak splitting and merging has been studied by various authors. Concerning the normal parametrisation Van Veen [Van Veen et al 1980] has deduced the relationships between feature dimensions, image space quantisation and parameter space quantisation. Niblack, [Niblack et al 1988], has used these results and extends them to cases of noisy images and obtains sub-accumulator-cell accuracy.

A recent new approach to the analysis of Hough space by Princen, Illingworth and Kittler [Princen et al 1990] considers the design of optimum one-dimensional filters which sharpen the peak structure in parameter space. This approach takes the view that the Hough Transform is a hypothesis testing mechanism where a statistical hypothesis is an assumption made about the distribution of a random variable. The statistical 'test' of a hypothesis is a procedure in which a sample of size n is used to determine whether the hypothesis may be rejected or accepted. A test statistic, T_n, is used to determine whether the observed data can be attributed to a particular distribution with a set of defining parameters Ω_0. This is called the *null* hypothesis. There is an accept/reject thresholding effect with a critical value, t, of the test statistic. The key to determining the performance of a test statistic is the power function which gives the probability of rejection as a function of the underlying parametric distribution of data points. Attempting to make the power function narrow is an approach to optimizing the performance of the Hough Transform. This leads to a redefinition of the Hough Transform in which the value at a point in the transform plane is a measure of the distribution of points around a curve rather than the number of points on a curve. In an illustrative model, concerning straight line detection, three parameters are made explicit. These are (p, θ), the normal parameters of the line, and w, a parameter specifying the distribution of points across the line. Tests on real data clearly demonstrate the sensitivity of the method to line width rather than length. This gives improvements in the detection of short but straight features and less confusion due to the accidental association of image points.

6.3 Software Solutions

As we already know, calculation of the Hough Transform cannot be considered in isolation. The total computational burden is spread across the three stages of pre-processing, transformation of data and postprocessing. It may be that an adjustment to any or all of these stages gives rise to a significant reduction in computational complexity. We will begin with the simplest solutions first.

6.3.1 Computer friendly algorithms

It may be that you are not fortunate enough to have access to any fancy hardware and do not have stringent targets concerning the run time of your algorithm but you really don't want to have to take a coffee break each time you run it. In this case what is needed is simply to use the hardware you have in the most efficient way possible. Perhaps the simplest methods of optimizing the calculation of the transformation involve re-writing the basic algorithm in a computer efficient form. Before we analyse anything in particular let's take a look at what computers can do and how long it takes them to do it.

To begin with, at the level of an actual calculation, all numbers are represented to the base two. That is, they are binary numbers. If we program our instructions using a decimal representation, this has an input/output conversion cost attached to it. In addition, the distinction exists between floating point arithmetic, and integer or whole number arithmetic. It is much quicker to perform arithmetic operations using integers than it is to perform them using floating point numbers. With this in mind, let's take a closer look at two particular algorithms.

The first algorithm reduces the number of necessary calculations by pre-calculating the required values and storing them in arrays which can be indexed by the image point co-ordinates. This is a universally applicable technique. A particular example of such an algorithm, [Leavers 1988c], is given Appendix 4. This is used to determine the normal parameters, (p, θ), of a straight line. While this method speeds up the computation, it introduces an extra cost concerning memory requirements.

A second computer-wise algorithm, the Binary Hough Transform (BHT), [Da Fontoura Costa et al 1989], uses a modified slope intercept parametrisation of the straight line. To implement this method, the dimensions of both the image and the transform space should be integer powers of two. The calculations can then be executed using only binary shifts and additions. Because this is the most efficient way of asking a computer to perform calculations it gives a significant saving in computation time. In addition the parameters can be represented exactly and integer arithmetic is used without rounding errors. A drawback of the technique is that it needs four two-dimensional transform planes.

121

6.3.2 Dynamically Quantised Accumulators

Quantisation of the Hough space is generally chosen to reflect the required accuracy in the determination of the individual parameters. However, the size of the accumulator has a direct effect on the computational cost of performing the transformation. If n parameters are under detection,each having T values, then an implementation of the SHT would require T^n memory allocations in order to maintain an n dimensional accumulator. Further to this, the incrementation stage requires T^{n-1} calculations per image point using the SHT.

When interpreting information in Hough space, it is clear that only those locations in the accumulator which exhibit a dense packing of relatively high values are of interest. Various authors have realized that memory requirements and computational load can be dramatically reduced using an intelligent iterative, *coarse to fine* accumulation technique. To do this, the accumulator is examined at various scales and an attempt is made to evaluate it in detail only in those areas having a high density of counts One of the first advocates of this strategy was Silberberg [Silberberg et al. 1984]. He used the method to determine the viewing parameters in three-dimensional object recognition.

The Fast Hough Transform, (FHT), of Li [Li et al 1985] uses the same strategy for straight line detection. The Hough space is partitioned into quadrants and accumulated. Each quadrant is then examined and the algorithm proceeds by subdivision at each scale of those quadrants containing votes in excess of a predetermined threshold. Quadrants are processed until they either fail to produce enough votes or reach a predetermined size. The FHT uses a fast incremental test in order to determine which image points vote for a quadrant. A disadvantage of the method is that it necessitates use of the slope intercept parametrisation and consequently two independent accumulators must be maintained for lines having gradients either greater or less than unity. In addition, the rigid quadtree decomposition of Hough space means that lines generating 'split peaks' which cross the boundaries of quadrants may be missed by the processing.

The Adaptive Hough Transform, (AHT) [Illingworth et al 1987] is a more flexible variation of the technique. It compensates for peak splitting by using a focusing mechanism. A 9×9 accumulator initially covers the full range of parameters. After accumulation candidate peaks are identified by thresholding and connected components analysis. The parameter limits covered by the accumulator array are then adjusted to focus on the most prominent peak. The cycle is then repeated.

Detailed investigation of the AHT shows that it suffers from a number of problems which make it inferior to the standard method under general conditions. In particular, the method cannot identify lines reliably, unless the number of lines is small and they are long with respect to the size of the image. Interested readers should follow the work of Princen who has produced papers concerning both the properties of the AHT, [Princen et al 1989a] and a comparison of the SHT, FHT and AHT methods [Princen et al 1989b].

6.3.3 Constraints on Parameter Calculation

Using the Hough transform, low level feature points generate evidence concerning all possible groupings of points within the image. The standard technique is computationally intensive because evidence is generated over a large range of possible parameter values. The computational load can be reduced by using information from the image to restrict the range of parameters which must be calculated for each image point. Edge direction information made available at the edge detection pre-processing stage is the most commonly used constraint on the range of parameters to be calculated.

Ballard [Ballard 1981] points out that circle detection may be optimised by the use of gradient information. Parameter generation is restricted to a single line on the surface of a cone in the three dimensional parameter space. Not only does this reduce the computational load associated with the calculation of the parameters but it also facilitates the postprocessing for peak detection.

In the case of the straight line detection, the edge direction is linked directly to the line gradient and, for the normal parametrisation, can be used to limit the range of θ over which the associated p values should be calculated [Leavers 1988c]. Again peak detection is made easier by the existence of a sparse accumulator. However, this approach requires an accurate estimation of the edge direction data. A large mask needs to be used in the edge detection stage, which merely shifts the computational burden.

While edge direction is the most commonly used information, curvature and grey level constraints have also been used in this way. For example, Hakalahti [Hakalahti et al 1984] has developed a method of two dimensional object recognition by matching local properties of contour points.

6.3.4 Parameter Space Decomposition

Where more than two parameters are under detection, standard parametric transformation may involve impractically large computation and storage requirements. To deal with this particular difficulty, a further class of methods decomposes the computation into separate stages, each stage passing results to the next. In this way a high dimensional problem is reduced to a series of lower dimensional problems. This leads to substantial savings, not only in storage requirements but also in the amount of calculation required.

We have already used a parameter reduction technique in chapter five, [Leavers 1988b]. We did this by considering the way in which curves map into the two dimensional parameter space used for straight line detection. A filtering of this first transform plane and a second transformation of this filtered data gave us the parameters associated with the circle.

Another alternative approach to circle detection uses edge direction information in order to reduce the dimensionality of the problem. Examples of such two stage methods are detailed in references [Illingworth et al 1987] and [Davies 1990]. Edge vectors are estimated using a standard Sobel operator. A normal to the tangent to the circle at the point (x, y) will pass through the centre of the circle and make an angle θ with the horizontal axis. The relationship between the data triples, (x, y, θ), and the centre co-ordinates, (x_0, y_0), is deduced. This allows the data triples to be mapped into a two-dimensional, (x_0, y_0), parameter space as straight lines. The intersection of many straight lines identifies the centre co-ordinates of the circle. These values are then used to calculate a histogram of possible radius values.

In the case of ellipse detection, Tsukune and Goto [Tsukune et al 1983] have shown that similar edge based constraints may be derived and used to decompose the five dimensional, single stage problem into three stages where each step determines at most two parameters. Yuen [Yuen et al 1988] has superseded this with a method that works in situations where the previous technique failed. The penalty paid for the increased efficiency at the transformation stage of the processing is that there is a reliance on good edge information. While edge detection using a large mask is a computationally intensive task, this can usually be traded off against the speed-up in run-time and reduced memory requirements. A disadvantage of the technique concerning performance is that a multistage process may introduce systematic errors which propagate through the various stages.

6.3.5 Segmenting the Image

In reference [Wallace 1985] segmentation of the image is considered. Segments of the same line contribute separately to the same entry in the transform space. But still all possible values of the dependent parameter are calculated. Segmenting the image in this case is equivalent to a reduction in resolution, which may not be acceptable.

Princen [Princen et al 1989] has introduced a hierarchical approach to line detection which uses a pyramidal method of image segmentation. At the lowest level of the pyramid short line segments are detected by applying a Hough Transform to small segments of the image. The algorithm proceeds by grouping line segments into longer lines. Line segments which have local support propagate up through the hierarchy and are grouped at higher levels. Thus the length of a line will determine the level of the pyramid to which it propagates. The method introduces a mechanism which relates the dimensions of the feature and the resolution of the representation.

6.4 Parallel Processing

What follows is a short introduction to parallel implementations of the Hough Transform which are mapped onto existing general purpose parallel systems. Such computer architectures may be used in one of two ways. The first is the 'Single Instruction Multiple Data' (SIMD) type. This consists of n processing elements (PE's) which each simultaneously perform the same operation on n independent pieces of data. In general many simple PE's are used. The second type of machine is the 'Multiple Instruction Multiple Data' (MIMD) in which processors simultaneously perform different sets of instructions on independent pieces of data. In contrast to the SIMD machines, MIMD systems are usually built out of a smaller number of faster processors and each PE needs to address a very large memory space. There are various ways in which the memory can be distributed. One way is for all n processors to share the same memory. In this case the major problem is memory access contention. A second way is for each processor to have a unique memory address space connected to a network with interprocessor links. In this case network congestion can be as bad or worse than congestion in access to a shared memory. For the interested reader an excellent, detailed survey of parallel implementations and architectures is given by Albanesi and Ferretti [Albanesi et al 1990].

6.4.1 SIMD Implementations

SIMD machines can be categorized according to the way in which the processing elements are configured. There are many possible configurations, four of which are linear, mesh, tree and pyramid.

A linear array will have n PE's with a linear interconnecting path in which each processor can communicate with its immediate neighbours to the right and to the left. A controller broadcasts instructions to each PE. The projection based Hough Transform has been implemented on a linear array configuration called the Scan Line Processor (SLAP) [Fisher 1986].

For image processing needs, e.g., edge detection operations, it is useful for each processor to be connected to its nearest neighbours both top and bottom as well as left and right. This configuration is called a Mesh-Connected SIMD machine. In such a machine the processors are arranged in a square lattice. Each PE is labelled according to its position in the lattice and can communicate with its four nearest neighbours. A fundamental problem exists in mapping the Hough Transform algorithm onto such architectures in that the accumulation stage of the transformation requires global shifting and summarization of the data from all parts of the mesh. For example, using the normal parametrisation, if the n pixels of an image each have a dedicated processor and each processor is broadcast a single value of θ together with $\sin\theta$ and $\cos\theta$, then it can calculate the appropriate value of $p = x\cos\theta + y\sin\theta$. Each processor will then have a value of p which needs to be accumulated with respect to all other similar values of p. Rosenfeld [Rosenfeld et al 1988] has studied various mappings of the Hough algorithm onto such machines. He concludes that whereas a Mesh-Connected SIMD machine is ideally suited to performing local operations on an image in parallel, they are not so well suited for operations that involve global communication. However, many mesh architectures do have special support for accumulation across the whole mesh.

A further type of SIMD system is the binary tree. This particular configuration allows greater flexibility in the kind of possible communication. Three types of communication are possible these are:

1.) Global bus communication which allows a datum to be broadcast from the controller or conversely from a single processor to the controller.

2.) Tree communication which exploits local connectivity and allows adjacent PE's to exchange data in parallel.

3.) Linear communications that reconfigures the whole tree into a linear array. Reference [Ibrahim et al 1986] details two algorithms implemented on a tree structured machine.

The last type of SIMD machine is the Pyramid. This type of configuration will support multi-resolution processing. It consists of a set of reduced resolution arrays of nodes arranged as a grid within each layer and augmented with hierarchical interconnections between adjacent layers. Both [Jolion et al 1989] and [Bongiovanni et al 1990] have reported implementations of the Hough algorithm on SIMD Pyramid machines. Of all the SIMD configurations the Pyramid is perhaps the most 'Hough Friendly'.

6.4.2 MIMD Implementations

The following parallel implementations of the Hough Transform on MIMD machines can be categorized according to the many ways in which the memory is shared or partitioned. Three such categories are:

1.) Input partioning.

2.) Output partioning.

3.) Mixed input/output partioning.

The first category causes the most severe form of contention. This is because in the accumulation stage of the algorithm the shared parameter space undergoes an updating process. This is viable only if the number of votes generated by each image point is very small. It is achievable in the case of straight line detection using the Modified Hough, (s_1, s_2), parametrisation [Wallace 1985]. Such an implementation, on a Butterfly Parallel Processor (BPP), is detailed in reference [Olson et al 1987].

The second type of memory partioning allows more alternatives concerning contention of access to image space memory. An algorithm which uses the (p, θ) normal parametrisation is detailed in [Olson et al 1987].

The third strategy of mixed output/input partioning requires extensive data transmission among the processors. It has been realized using a carefully designed interprocessor communications protocol [Ben-Tzvi et al 1989] on an Overlapped Shared Memory Multiprocessor Architecture or OSSMA system.

6.5 Dedicated Hardware

In general, such systems are developed with a single application in mind. The design is often constrained by the cost and performance specifications of the application. It is not appropriate to review such implementations here as they require much specialized knowledge. The interested reader should refer to Albanesi and Ferretti, [Albanesi et al 1990].

6.6 The Probabilistic Houghs: A Review

It is clear that while the Hough technique is a promising approach to the important task of shape detection in computer vision, many problems still deter its application in real-life systems. Using a Standard Hough Transform (SHT) algorithm, each image point votes independently for all instances of the shape under detection on which it may lie. In this way a great redundancy of evidence concerning the image is generated. A new genre of Hough-like techniques has appeared in the recent [Kiryati et al 1991], [Bergen et al 1991], [Xu et al 1990], [Califano et al 1989] and [Leavers 1990], the Probabilistic Hough Transforms (PHT's). These techniques seek to reduce the generation of redundant evidence by sampling the image data in various ways. They are able to reduce significantly the run-time of the technique. In addition the algorithms deal with binary edge data and do not depend on computationally expensive global preprocessing of the image. They are unique in that each has the potential to detect n parameters.

The following illustrated review traces a logical developmental sequence through the various methods. It is ordered on the potential reduction in the calculation of redundant information offered by each method. Thus, the sequence is not chronological and each method has evolved independently of any other. It is not intended that the methods be evaluated with respect to each other. This would be unfair as each method may offer very substantial computational savings in a particular application. Where comparisons are made, a very simple rule of thumb is used; that the algorithms should perform at least as well as the SHT under given conditions.

In order to compare the differences between the various techniques and using the normal parametrisation:

$$p = x \cos \theta + y \sin \theta \qquad (1)$$

an example of the computation of the Standard Hough Transform of a simple $N \times N$ image, $(N = 128)$, is shown in Fig. 6.1 . The image, shown as an inset, contains two long lines and one short line. There are a total of 643 points of which 294 are due to the three lines and the remainder are due to random Gaussian noise. The transform plane of this image is shown as two surface plots. These are defined in the ranges $\theta[0, \pi]$, (quantized in steps of $\Delta \theta = \pi/N$) and $p[-N/2, N/2]$, (quantized in steps of $\Delta p = 1$). The larger plot has an elevation angle of 25° and the smaller plot an elevation angle of 10°. Clearly visible are the three isolated peaks whose locus corresponds to the parameters of the three straight lines in the image. The heights of the peaks correspond to the length of the lines they represent. While it appears that a simple thresholding technique will determine the three sets of (p, θ) parameters, in practice we have seen, that where multiple features of differing dimensions are under detection, simply searching for local maxima and thresholding is not sufficient. Where necessary, peak detection was achieved following the method detailed in chapter 4 which convolves the transform plane with a matched filter and thresholds the result.

Kiryati et al [Kiryati et al 1991] point out that the incrementation stage of the SHT usually dominates the execution time of the algorithm. They have proposed a probabilistic algorithm in which the image data are randomly sampled and only the sampled subset of image points is transformed. The results are accumulated in the normal way. It is shown that a threshold effect exists concerning the behaviour of the number of false peaks detected as a function of sample size. It is concluded that as the complexity of the image increases, the sample size must also correspondingly increase. The method was applied to the image shown in Fig. 6.1 . The method of peak detection of chapter 4 was used and thresholded at the lowest value indicative of a genuine line in the image. At a 10% sampling level there were very many false peaks. At a 20% sampling level this had dropped to 7 and at 24% to just 1. Fig. 6.2 shows the result of this sampling at 24%. Inset is the image formed by the sampled subset of points. The false peak shown is due to a line of disconnected noise points in the image which is discernible by eye. This effect persisted until a 35% sample of points was taken. A graph of this thresholding effect is shown in Fig. 6.3 . This algorithm will introduce savings in the calculation and accumulation stages of the processing that depend on the quality and type of image data. Memory requirements remain unchanged.

The probabilistic techniques of Xu et al [Xu et al 1990], Leavers et al [Leavers et al 1989], Bergen et al [Bergen et al 1991] and Califano et al [Califano et al 1989], while they differ in many respects all share a common feature, they all map sets of n

127

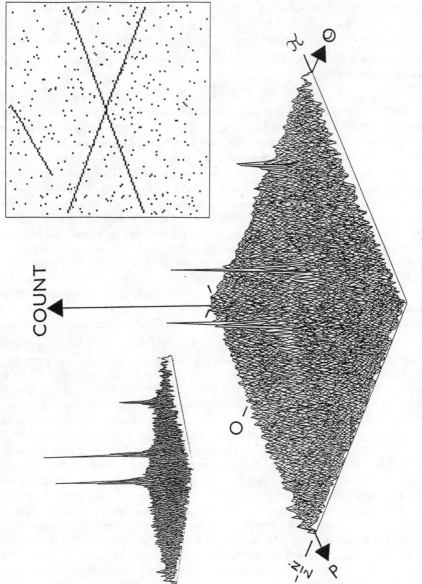

COUNT

Fig 6.1 *Standard Hough Transform*

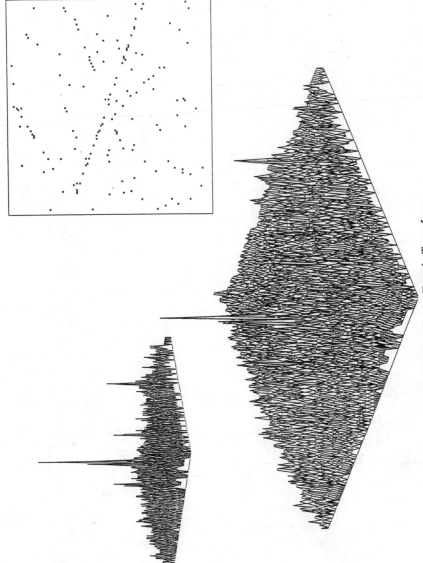

Fig 6.2 *Probabilistic Hough Transform*

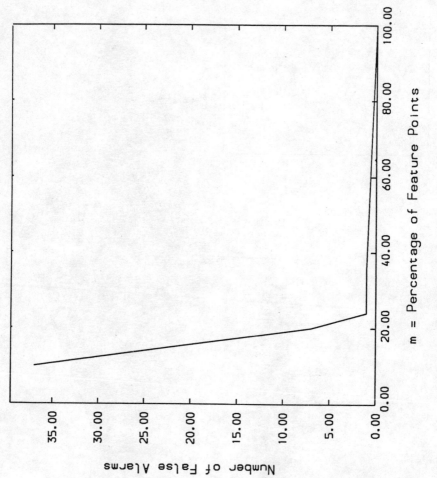

m = Percentage of Feature Points

Fig 6.3 *Graph showing thresholding effect*

130

image points into just one point in the transform space. In this way the image data vote for the most probable as opposed to all possible instances of the shape under detection. Votes accumulate in the areas of the transform plane associated with the highest probabilities of feature instance. This does much to reduce the effects of bias caused by correlated noise effects in the transform space.

Sampling sets of n image points gives rise a combinatorially explosive number of possible sets. Xu et al [Xu et al 1990] do not refer to this problem explicitly. They do however solve it by the use of a dynamic algorithm, that is, sampling stops when a predetermined threshold count is accumulated. The parameters associated with that high count are used to identify and remove from the image the feature indicated. When a feature is removed from the image the accumulator or its equivalent is reset to zero and the process begins again. The authors do not give any absolute criterion for determining the necessary threshold. Using this method, the transform space will be sparse. Because of this, the authors suggest that it is not necessary to maintain a standard n dimensional accumulator table in which to store the results of the transformation but rather to create a set P in which each element contains both a real valued function and an integer score to implicitly represent the transform space. P is updated at each step by the point mapped from a randomly picked set of pixels. In order to reduce the complexity of search associated with the suggested data structure a linked list method is suggested. Similarly, previous work has shown that a reduction in search space complexity can be achieved by keeping a suitably constructed Hash table [Brown et al 1983]. However, systematic distortion, occlusion and feature perturbation are known to pose difficult problems for such methods of accumulation [Brown et al 1983]. Moreover, the difficulties of constructing a linked list or Hash table where the number of parameters under detection exceeds two are not dealt with.

The method was applied to the image shown in Fig. 6.1 . Step one searches the image for feature points and stores those points as a list F. In step two, sets of two points are chosen at random from the list F such that any point has an equal probability of being chosen. Step three uses equation (1) to simultaneously solve for the (p, θ) parameters defining the line on which both points are situated. Xu et al [Xu et al 1990] do not suggest any stopping criteria by which to determine the optimum number of samples to be taken. In the absence of such a predetermined stopping criterion, it was decided to use a threshold of 10. The shortest line in the image was of length 44 points. In order to illustrate to the reader the way in which the algorithm reduces the generation of redundant information, the results were accumulated in the normal way. In addition, a check was kept for each run of the algorithm to determine how many cells were accumulated and how many two point sets were sampled before a threshold value of 10 was accumulated in any cell thus simulating the results of reference [Xu et al 1990]. The results are shown in Fig. 6.4 . The first two runs were very efficient. In the first run, the number of sampled sets or trials was 466 and the number of cells accumulated was 424. The peak associated with a long line in the image is very clearly distinct. Similarly the second line was detected after 268 sets were sampled and only 251 cells were accumulated. However, the third run shows that it would be impossible for the algorithm to detect the shortest line. This run was terminated after 2,500 sampling trials had failed to produce a maximum count of 10. There are simply too many other phantom lines in the image caused by the

131

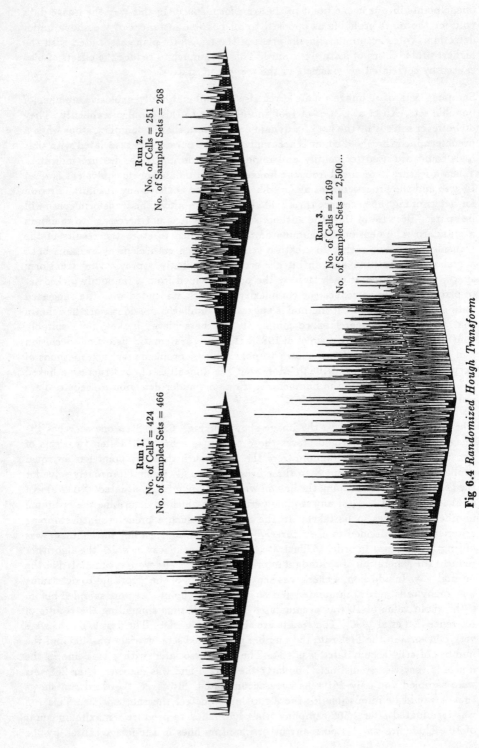

Run 1.
No. of Cells = 424
No. of Sampled Sets = 466

Run 2.
No. of Cells = 251
No. of Sampled Sets = 268

Run 3.
No. of Cells = 2169
No. of Sampled Sets = 2,500...

Fig 6.4 *Randomized Hough Transform*

aggregation of disconnected noise points.

Bergen and Shvaytser [Bergen et al 1991] have produced a strictly theoretical paper. In it they suggest a Monte-Carlo approximation to the Hough transform. Three algorithms are suggested the first of which approximates to that of Kiryati et al. A further two algorithms are suggested which are equivalent to the RHT of Xu et al also discussed above. Their analysis, while mathematically rigorous and complete, deals only with single feature, noiseless data and there is no suggestion as to future publications concerning implementations.

Both Leavers et al [Leavers et al 1989] and Califano et al [Califano et al 1989] recognize and make explicit the problems concerning the combinatorial explosiveness inherent in their respective techniques. Both suggest segmenting the image in some way. Califano et al use a method of 'Generalized Neighbourhoods'. Circular segments are swept out around fixed feature points. Constraints are imposed on the size and location of the segments. Successive segments must overlap and their size is chosen such that the radius of the circle is that distance over which two neighbourhoods are expected to contain coherent information. Califano et al use a traditional n dimensional accumulator and point out the difficulties in interpreting the accumulated evidence which are associated with the effects of correlated noise. To find an overall consistent interpretation of the data, they use a 'competitive integration' mechanism motivated by connectionist networks.

The next chapter gives a detailed account of the Dynamic Generalized Hough Transform DGHT [Leavers 1990, 1991]. The algorithm incorporates features which have been introduced in previous suggested approaches and shares some features with the other PHT's. It does, however, differ from other SHT and PHT algorithms in two fundamental ways. The first difference is that the algorithm selects a single connected point, (x_c, y_c), and uses this point to seed the transformation. The n parameters associated with the shape under detection are calculated using (x_c, y_c) together with sets of $(n-1)$ randomly sampled image points. In this way voting is constrained to be on the hypersurface in transform space which would be generated by the standard transformation of (x_c, y_c). The algorithm maps each set of n image points to a single point on this surface. Voting is further restricted by appropriate segmentation of the image data. The second fundamental difference exploits the production of a sparse transform space by projecting the results of the transformation onto the axes of the n dimensional transform space. Hence if T is the resolution in transform space and n is the number of parameters under detection then use of the DGHT reduces memory requirements from T^n to nT and introduces the opportunity for parallel calculation and accumulation of parameters.

Thus, in the present case of straight line detection, the connected point, (x_c, y_c), is paired with i other sampled feature points in the image in order to determine the θ parameter of the line connecting such pairs of points:

$$\theta = \tan^{-1}\left(-\frac{(x_c - x_i)}{(y_c - y_i)}\right) \qquad (2)$$

This constrains the location of the voting in transform space to be along the sinusoid generated by substituting (x_c, y_c) into equation (1) . The effect is shown in Fig. 6.5 . The θ histogram is shown as an inset. Once sufficient image points have been

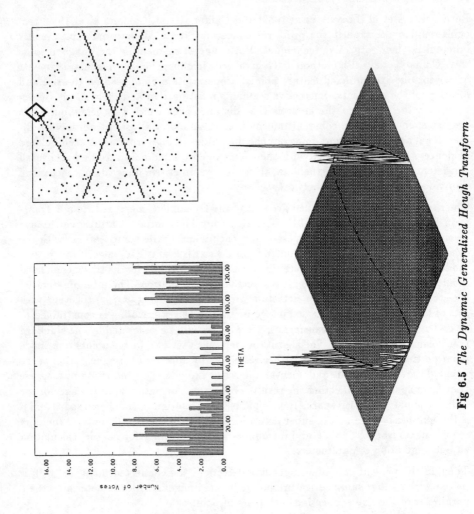

Fig 6.5 *The Dynamic Generalized Hough Transform*

sampled, the histogram is searched to determine the maximum number of votes at location θ_0. The associated p_0 may be calculated by substitution of (x_c, y_c) and θ_0 into equation (1) . The line is then removed from the image and the processing begins again after re-intialization of the one dimensional accumulator.

Essential to the efficient use of the probabilistic techniques are stopping criteria which ensure adequate sampling with respect to the desired detection result and which also give optimum computational savings. A robust stopping criterion has been deduced for the DGHT [Leavers 1990]. In the case study presented in the next chapter this is applied to the concurrent detection of circles and ellipses using real image data over a range and variety of noise conditions. It is shown that the DGHT copes well with both occlusion and the effects of correlated noise. In addition, the method provides an efficient feedback mechanism linking the accumulated boundary point evidence and the contributing boundary point data. It achieves this goal automatically with an intelligent monitoring of the transformation.

CHAPTER 7

A Case Study:
Circles and Ellipses

One of the most striking things concerning the plethora of literature relating to computationally realistic implementations of the Hough Transform is that the majority of effort is directed towards straight line detection. Such implementations can seldom be generalized to include the detection of shapes having more than two defining parameters. Moreover, the detection of more complicated shapes is rarely dealt with other than by the use of software solutions. The Probabilistic Houghs offer a unique opportunity for generalization to n dimensions. In particular, the Dynamic Generalized Hough Transform has an algorithm that is uniquely suited to parallel implementation irrespective of the number of parameters under detection.

The following is a detailed illustrative application of the technique to real image data. It is intended to evaluate the method by simulating the conditions which might reasonably exist in an industrial environment, variable lighting conditions, shadows, reflections from the objects and damaged or occluded objects. The automatic inspection of food and confectionery is a standard industrial inspection task. Accordingly such a subject was chosen for this case study. The objects under detection are chocolates, in particular circular and elliptical chocolates. Thus, we develop an algorithm for the concurrent detection of circles and ellipses. This is not a difficult task as the circle is simply a limiting case of the ellipse. The algorithm has much wider applications as circles become ellipses when rotated about an axis perpendicular to the viewing angle and this is a common occurrence in many computer vision situations. Let's first take a look at the necessary preprocessing.

7.1 Preprocessing the Image Data

The real image of some Viennese Chocolate Truffles is shown in Fig. 7.1 . As we cannot use this image directly, we need first to edge-detect and then to threshold the edge-detected image in order to provide the binary input data required by the transformation process. We can edge detect by convolution with a simple five point Laplacian of the form

$$\mathbf{L} = \begin{bmatrix} 0 & 1 & 0 \\ 1 & -4 & 1 \\ 0 & 1 & 0 \end{bmatrix}$$

The resulting grey level image is shown in Fig. 7.2 .

Why use this particular operator? Firstly, we are here detecting curved shapes and the Laplacian operator has the nice property of being isotropic, that is, it is orientation independent. Secondly, the 3×3 window size and the fact that it requires only one multiplication and four additions make it computationally trivial and fast to apply.

All that now remains is to determine a threshold in order to binarize the edge image. As this is an arbitrarily chosen parameter, we need to consider the range of threshold values within which we can reasonably expect the algorithm to cope. In addition we need to know how critical the choice of threshold is. This is because in real computer vision situations unanticipated changes may occur in the quality of the image data, for example, due to variations in the lighting conditions. We need to develop an algorithm which can cope with such changes without substantial degradation of the results of processing. To test the robustness of the algorithm with respect to perturbations in this threshold, the edge image was thresholded at 60%, 50% and 45% of its intensity range. The results are shown in Fig. 7.3 . It can be seen that the sugar crystals on the chocolates cause noise points to appear as speckles on the chocolate surface in the binary images. This effect degrades as the threshold is reduced but the boundaries of the objects are also correspondingly degraded.

Now that we have our input data, let's go on to look in some detail at the Dynamic Generalized Hough Transform (DGHT) algorithm.

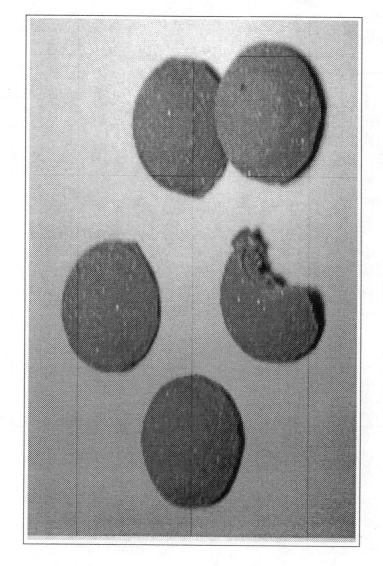

Fig 7.1 Real image of Viennese Chocolate truffles

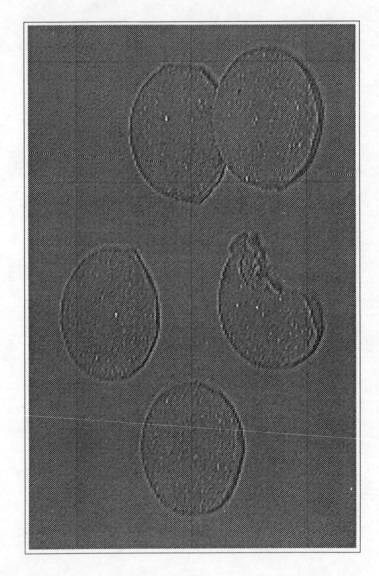

Fig 7.2 *Image after Laplacian Edge Detection Operation*

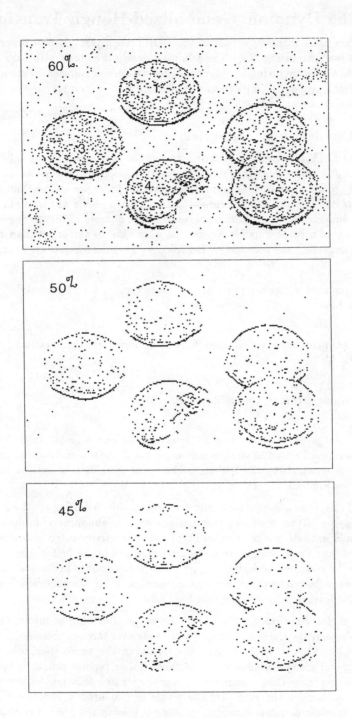

Fig 7.3 *Range of Thresholds for Edge Image*

7.2 The Dynamic Generalized Hough Transform

This section deals with the details of the DGHT algorithm. A flow diagram of the algorithm is shown in Fig. 7.4 . The following description deals with each successive stage of the algorithm giving both general information and sufficient particular details to enable the reader to implement the algorithm with respect to the concurrent detection of circles and ellipses.

7.2.1 Connectivity Detection

Using the DGHT, processing begins by scanning the edge image for a single connected feature point. To do this, an initial constraint is imposed that over a 3×3 neighbourhood around a point, that point is connected if there are no less than 2 adjacent feature points. Isolated noise points or pairs of noise points are thus eliminated in this first simple check. In addition, because of the discrete nature of the image, the connectivity of a point may be categorized according to the orientation of the line segment connecting the point to its neighbours. Three categories are suggested:

a) A line segment whose orientation, θ, is more vertical then horizontal.
$45° \leq \theta < 135°$.

b) A line segment whose orientation, θ, is more horizontal then vertical.
$-45° \leq \theta < 45°$.

c) A line segment that is exactly diagonal.

In the present work, it is required to detect circles and ellipses. In digital images, such shapes have horizontal straight line segments at the top and bottom and vertical straight line segments to the left and right. This remains true even if an ellipse is rotated. See Fig. 7.5 .

In view of this, once a candidate connected point is selected using the 3×3 adjacency test, it may be further tested by summation over a neighbourhood around the point which would indicate one of the three types of connectivity listed above. Because it is assumed that whole shapes are under detection and in the first instance the image is scanned by rows, left to right, it is appropriate to consider horizontal connectivity first. This is achieved by summing the number of points in the neighbourhood around a candidate feature point as shown in Fig. 7.6 .

However, if, for some reason, the top of the shape is missing or incomplete, then a vertical connectivity check can be similarly made over the neighbourhood illustrated in Fig. 7.7 . Clearly, in each case, the results of the summation over the 3×3 neighbourhood are still available and so horizontal or vertical connectivity detection entails nothing more than a summation over the six new locations of the neighbourhood. In both cases the sum over the whole neighbourhood should be ≥ 4. The check for absolute diagonal connectivity was not used in the present context of circle and ellipse detection.

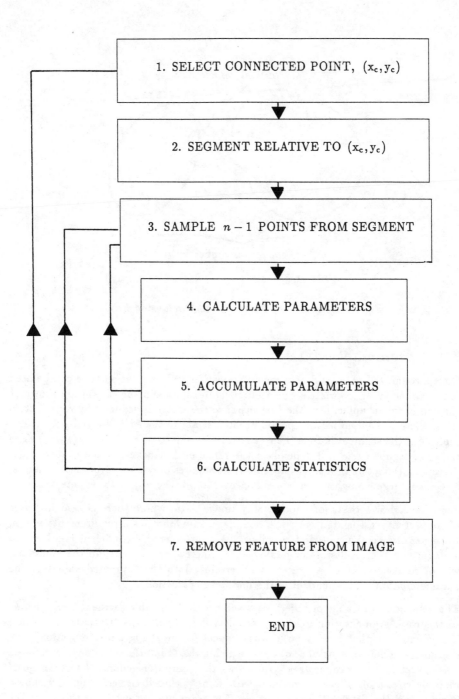

1. SELECT CONNECTED POINT, (x_c, y_c)

2. SEGMENT RELATIVE TO (x_c, y_c)

3. SAMPLE $n - 1$ POINTS FROM SEGMENT

4. CALCULATE PARAMETERS

5. ACCUMULATE PARAMETERS

6. CALCULATE STATISTICS

7. REMOVE FEATURE FROM IMAGE

END

Fig 7.4 *Flow Diagram of Dynamic Generalized Hough Transform Algorithm*

143

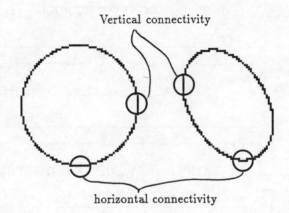

Vertical connectivity

horizontal connectivity

Fig 7.5 *Connectivity Particular to Circles and Ellipses*

7.2.2 Segmentation

Once a connected point is determined, its location and orientation type can be used to determine an appropriate segmentation. For example, in the case study shown at the end of this chapter, if in the first instance the image is scanned by rows, left to right, there will be no feature points of interest above the first selected point. The top row of the segment is thus the row containing the connected point, (x_c, y_c). The choice of segment size will depend on the range of dimensions of the shapes under detection. Detection of a single size of object requires only one segment size, that is, a segment large enough to contain sufficient data for the object to be detected.

Tests have shown that, for good quality image data, where there is a high degree of connectivity associated with the boundary, minimum data requirements are on the order of a semi-arc of circle or ellipse. A quarter arc is insufficient and leads to ambiguity in the results. Poor quality data, where there are gaps in the boundary, will of course introduce a degree of uncertainty into the estimated values of the parameters that is independent of the method of detection.

The detection of a range of object sizes will require a flexible segmentation scheme. In this case, segmentation follows a 'smallest first' rule. This is necessary because a segmentation, that is very large with respect to the shape under detection, may contain more than one instance of a shape giving rise to interference due to correlated noise effects. For example, Fig. 7.8 shows the computer generated test image of multiple circles of differing sizes and with some occluded circles. Fig. 7.9 shows, in mid-grey, the detected circles and also the segmentation used. In this case, the smallest segment size was chosen to be in the middle of the range of possible diameters of the circles. As can be seen in Fig. 7.9 , this is sufficiently large to detect all of the

144

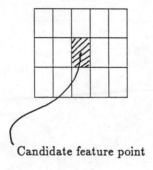

Candidate feature point

Fig 7.6 *Horizontal Neighbourhood*

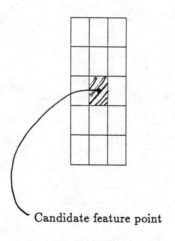

Candidate feature point

Fig 7.7 *Vertical Neighbourhood*

145

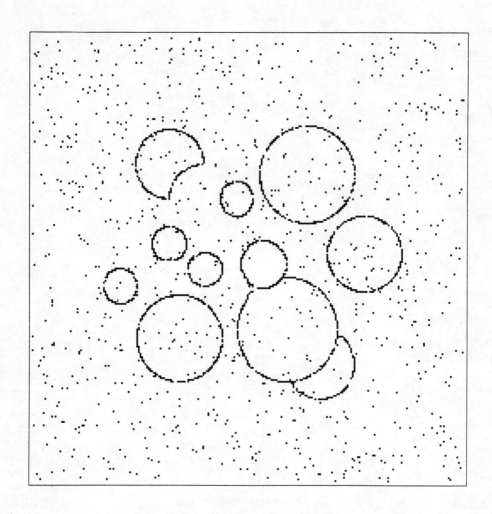

Fig 7.8 *Degraded Test Image*

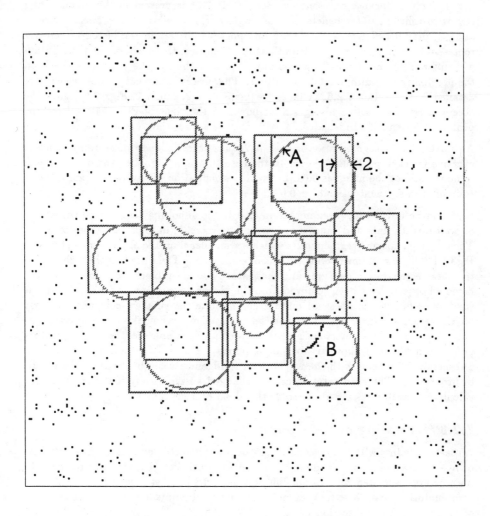

Fig 7.9 *Segmentation and detected Circles*

small and medium sized circles.

In addition, the algorithm is able to detect when there is insufficient data. The histogram on the left of Fig. 7.10 is for the rejected estimate of the radius of the circle **A** shown in Fig. 7.9 . This estimate was the result of transforming the points shown in the smaller segment labelled **1** in Fig. 7.9 . The histogram shows wide multiple peaks. This is because only one quarter circular arc is present in the segment and this is insufficient data to determine a single circle on which the connected point, (x_c, y_c), may lie. There is more than one possible circle and the histogram clearly represents a composition of distributions. In this case, the mean of the distribution will differ from the modal or maximum value and this can be used as a check on the possibility of multimodal distributions. The process of acceptance or rejection is detailed in subsection 7.2.6. A larger segment size (segment **2**, Fig. 7.9) gave the accepted estimate whose histogram is shown on the right of Fig. 7.10 . Here the peak is well defined and isolated.

An advantage of segmentation is that it reduces the signal to noise ratio which is effective for each particular shape. In the case shown in Fig. 7.9 , the overall signal to noise ratio of the image is 0.64, but with segmentation the average signal to noise ratio of each segment was 0.87 ± 0.08.

It should be noted that a segmentation that is too small may compound the effects of poor quality data and cause a corresponding increase in uncertainty of detection. The effect of choosing segment sizes which are smaller than the object size is shown in Fig. 7.11 . The real image on the left is of some coins. The image on the right shows the detected shapes in mid-grey and the feature points (in black) remaining after the detected objects have been removed from the binary edge image. As can be seen, the smallest segment size does not quite accommodate the smallest coin and similarly for the larger segment size. This has the effect of increasing the uncertainty in the detection of the parameters because the algorithm does not 'see' the missing feature points and fits only those 'visible' data points. This is of course an illustration. Subsection 7.2.6 deals with the way in which judgements can be made on the results of processing. The segmentation can be changed automatically if the errors in the calculated parameters are above some threshold of acceptability.

7.2.3 Sampling of data points

All feature points within a designated segment are detected and stored as a list. Sets of $n - 1$ data points are randomly sampled from this list. Clearly, to calculate the parameters associated with all possible sets of points in a list of length M would be a combinatorially explosive task. Hence only m sets of points are sampled. The choice of m is detailed in subsection 7.2.6

7.2.4 Calculating the Parameters

The DGHT may potentially be used to determine the n parameters associated with any analytically defined shape. However, each implementation requires careful consideration, in particular with respect to a suitable parametrization. Algorithms concerning the detection of straight lines and circles [Leavers et al 1989] and three-dimensional planes [Leavers 1990] have already been presented. The following details the calculation of the parameters associated with the concurrent detection of circles

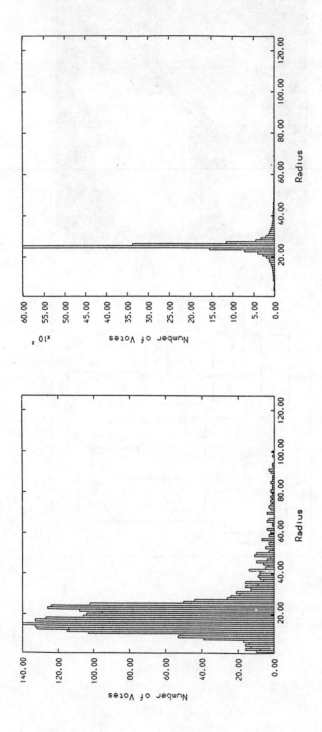

Fig 7.10 *Histograms of Rejected and Accepted Processing*

149

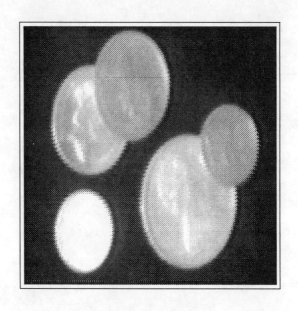

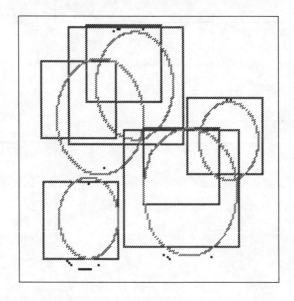

Fig 7.11 *Effect of Incorrect Segmentation*

and ellipses.

Using the DGHT, it may not always be possible to calculate directly the parameters of interest. In the first instance, it is important to choose a well determined, numerically stable model. A suitable equation with respect to the detection of ellipses is given in reference [Forbes 1987]:

$$x^2 + y^2 - U(x^2 - y^2) - V2xy - Rx - Sy - T = 0 \tag{1}$$

If (x_0, y_0) are the center co-ordinates of the ellipse, a and b its major and minor axes respectively and α the angle of rotation, then the ellipse eccentricity is given by $e = b/a$ and

$$U = \cos 2\alpha \frac{1 - e^2}{1 + e^2} \tag{2}$$

$$V = \sin 2\alpha \frac{1 - e^2}{1 + e^2} \tag{3}$$

$$R = 2x_0(1 - U) - 2y_0 V \tag{4}$$

$$S = 2y_0(1 + U) - 2x_0 V \tag{5}$$

$$T = \frac{2a^2 b^2}{a^2 + b^2} - \frac{x_0 R}{2} - \frac{y_0 S}{2} \tag{6}$$

U and V depend only on α and e. In particular, for a circle, U and V are zero. The discrete nature of the image representation means that, in general, in the case of a circle U and V will only approach zero. This case can be detected and the processing redirected to optimize the computation. Hence, for images which may contain both circles and ellipses such a mixture may be detected with a single scan of the image.

The ellipse parameters associated with each set of one connected point, (x_c, y_c) and four other randomly sampled points are calculated using the Gaussian elimination method with back substitution. A circular object will give rise to a singular matrix which is detected by a (near) zero pivot element. When this occurs, the processing is redirected as for a circle, i.e. using sets of three points to determine the parameters associated with a circle.

7.2.5 Accumulation of the Parameters

Correct use of the DGHT generates a very sparse transform space. This potentially allows the results of the transformation to be projected onto the n axes of the transform space. Votes are thus accumulated in n one-dimensional accumulators giving a very significant saving in memory requirements. In order to determine whether it is possible to accumulate in this way, a careful choice must be made of the parametric equation defining the accumulated parameters. As we saw in chapter six, in the case of the normal parametrization of the straight line

$$p = x \cos \theta + y \sin \theta$$

votes are restricted to be along a cosine curve. In this case, it is not possible to project the function onto the p axis. This is because p is not single valued; the cosine curve folds back on itself. A change of parametrization to $y = mx + c$ will restrict voting to occur only along a straight line in transform space, thus both m and c will be single valued. However, things are not so simple in the case of more than two-dimensions. For example, in Cartesian co-ordinates, the equation of a circle is given by:

$$(x - x_0)^2 + (y - y_0)^2 = r^2 \tag{7}$$

where (x_0, y_0) are the centre co-ordinates of the circle and r its radius. If we use equation (7) to execute the transformation to detect a circle, each feature point will generate points on the surface of a cone in a three-dimensional image space. See Fig. 7.12 . For a given radius, r, a circle is swept out around the point. This circle is the locus of all possible centres of circles of radius r on which the point, say (x_c, y_c), may be located. If it is desired that the DGHT accumulates the projections of this three-dimensional function onto the x_0, y_0 and r axes, it is necessary to somehow restrict the generation of evidence in the transform space such that the results are single valued with respect to all of the parameters under detection. This is done by the method of segmentation outlined in subsection 7.2.2. Segmenting in this way restricts the locus of votes in the transform space to one quarter of the surface of the cone which would be generated by a standard transformation of the connected point (x_c, y_c). The same was found to be effective for the detection of ellipses.

It may be that it is not convenient to accumulate the calculated parameters as in the present case of the concurrent detection of circles and ellipses. Thus, for each iteration, the calculated parameters U, V, R, S and T were used to obtain x_0, y_0, a, b and α and these became the accumulated parameters.

7.2.6 Statistical Information and a Robust Stopping Criterion

Where it is certain that only one object is under detection, the method will work well. However, interference may be generated as a result of the occlusion of an object or the effect of noise. When this happens, it is possible for the algorithm to detect such a failure by using the statistical information, governed by the binomial distribution, present in the one-dimensional accumulators associated with each parameter. For example, two sets of histograms are shown in Fig. 7.13 . The binary images from which they were generated are shown as insets. The two histograms on the left correspond to processing 'good' data. This consists of one object and relatively little noise. As can be seen, the histogram for the minor axis parameter b has a sharp well defined peak and the width of the distribution (a measure of the standard deviation) is narrow. Similarly, this can also be seen for the histogram corresponding to the y center co-ordinate. In contrast 'poor' data, consisting of a noisy image and occluded object, produce histograms where the peaks are not sharp and the standard deviations associated with the distributions are large compared to those associated with 'good' data.

In order to investigate the behaviour of the statistical information available in each of the five accumulators corresponding to the 5 ellipse parameters, the accumulators were examined at intervals of 500 over the range of $[(0), (14, 000)]$ sampled sets of four points. The graphs associated with the results of the processing are shown in the sequence of Figs. 7.14 - 7.16 . The binary test images are shown as insets. On the horizontal axis, the graphs show the number of sampling trials. Values along the

152

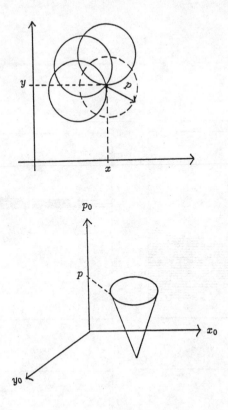

Fig 7.12 *Three-Dimensional Transform of circle*

vertical axis are in the range $[0, 180]$ as this is the range (in degrees) of the angle of rotation and also accommodates the ranges of values associated with the other parameters. The information shown in each graph corresponds to the distribution associated with the one-dimensional accumulator corresponding to that particular parameter. The variables shown are:

1. The modal value ◯

2. The mean - - - -

3. The standard deviation △

4. Number of votes at modal value (expectation value) ◇

153

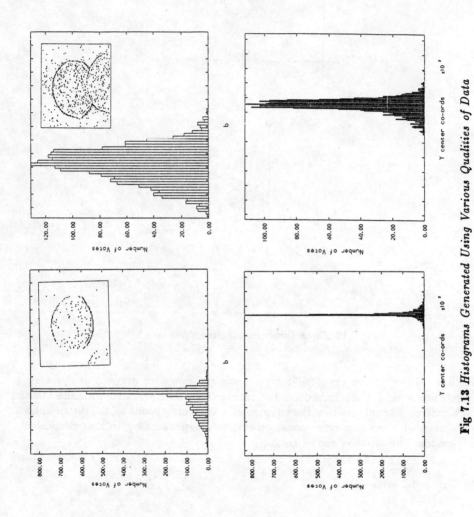

Fig 7.13 *Histograms Generated Using Various Qualities of Data*

154

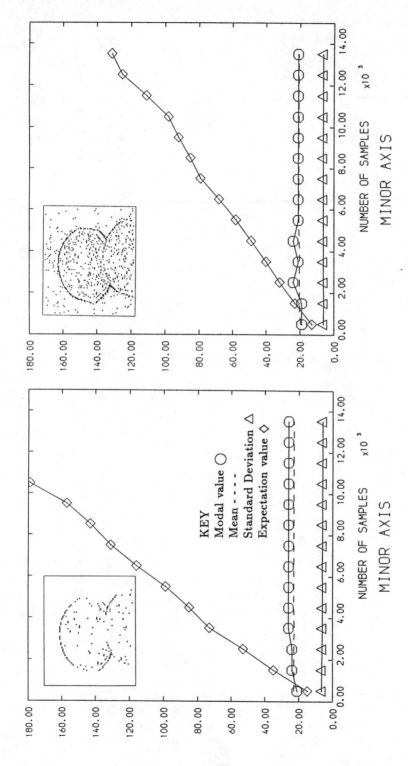

Fig 7.14 *Graphs for Minor Axis*

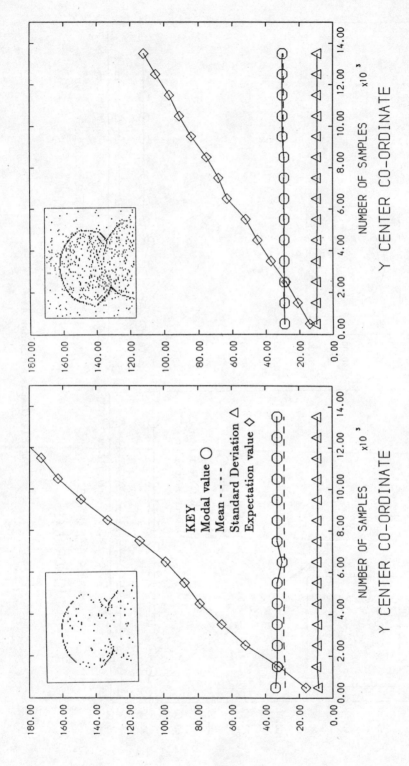

Fig 7.15 *Graphs for Y Centre Co-ordinate*

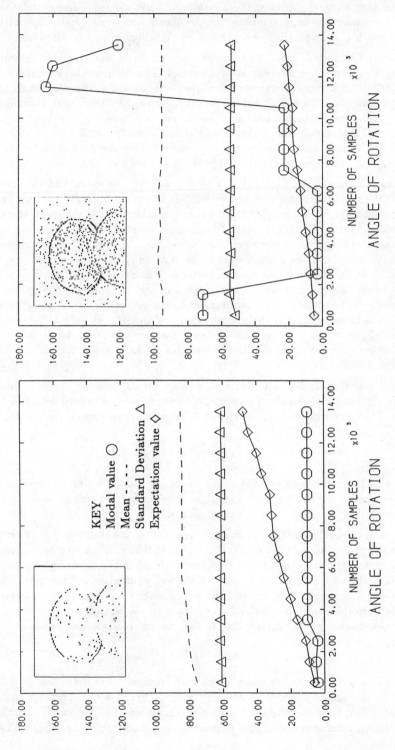

Fig 7.16 *Graphs for Angle of Rotation*

As can be seen from the graphs, the behaviour of the plotted values is relatively uniform over this very large sampling range. The values are an indication of the extent to which the distribution is corrupted by occlusion or structured noise.

Both objects are occluded and this causes an increase in the standard deviation indicating the composition of multiple distributions. The difference between the mean of the distribution and the modal value (i.e. the value located at the maximum count in the histogram) is also a measure of the extent to which the distribution is corrupted by noise or multiple instances of shape. In the case of a single unoccluded object, the mean and the modal value of the distribution associated with a parameter will converge after a sufficiently large number of trials. Where the data are insufficient, excessively noisy or there are multiple objects, this is not the case.

In the cases illustrated in Fig. 7.14 , and Fig. 7.15 , the mean and the modal values for the minor axis and y center co-ordinate of the noisy example on the right converge after approximately 4,500 trials have been taken. Those shown on the left, corresponding to the less noisy image, do not converge at all. This is because, even though the one image is much noisier than the other, the effect of the extra noise points in the vicinity of the missing edge at the bottom of the ellipse is to allow the missing edge to be filled in giving a much better estimate of b and y_0 than is possible for the 'cleaner' image. However, for the noisier image, the rotation is very poorly determined over the whole range of sampling and does not settle down to any constant value. This is because the noise points are causing many possible orientations of the estimated ellipses to be generated. In contrast, the 'cleaner' image has a much less variable estimate of the angle of rotation and this settles down to a constant value after about 2,500 trials.

The standard deviations associated with each image are larger in the case of the noisy image. In the case of the angle of rotation, α, the very large standard deviation is a function of the eccentricity, e, of the ellipse. That is, the variance of α depends on

$$\frac{1 + e^2}{1 - e^2} \tag{8}$$

Thus as $e \to 1$, corresponding to the ellipse becoming more circular, the variance of α increases, reflecting the fact that the angle is becoming less well defined. In this particular case, $a = 31$ and $b = 25$. This gives a value of $e = 0.81$.

Because of the combinatorial explosiveness inherent in the technique, it is crucial that, for the algorithm to work efficiently, it should 'know' when to stop sampling. A robust, automatic stopping criterion may be deduced in the following way. Using the DGHT, the expectation value of a parameter, η, is given by the product of the number of sampling trials, m, and the probability, f, that $n - 1$ points chosen randomly from the image data will all be situated on the boundary of the shape on which the connected point, (x_c, y_c), lies. In the case of an ellipse this becomes

$$\eta_e = m f_e^4 \tag{9}$$

If there is one to one correspondence between the number of sampled sets of points situated on the ellipse under detection and the number of votes accumulated in a given histogram, then the number of votes accumulated at a particular parameter value is the expectation value of that parameter (in practise this may differ with the

158

quantisation of the parameters or the width of the curve in image space). Thus, the fraction of the processed image points, represented by f_e, situated on the detected curve can be estimated from the gradient of the line generated by plotting the maximum count in the accumulator, η_e, against the number of sampling trials, m. As can be seen from Fig 7.14 , Fig. 7.15 and Fig. 7.16 , the gradient of the line is lower in the case of 'poor' quality data and indicates that a larger number of trials must be made to give a reliable result. The graphs of expectation value against sampling trials are approximately linear over the whole range tested. This means that the optimum sampling rate can be deduced after relatively few sampling trials.

To produce the results illustrated in the case study detailed in this chapter, the image data were sampled and processed to produce 200 accumulated estimates of the ellipse parameters. The histograms were then examined and the five maxima located. This was repeated five times. That is, five expectation values per parameter over a range of 1,000 trials were used to estimate the fraction, f_e, of image points contributing to the detected shape. In practice these values vary for each parameter and the lowest value is taken. The estimated fractional contribution, f_e, is then used to determine the number of trials needed to give as reliable an estimate of the parameters as the image data will allow. To do this, an expectation value, η_{opt}, which is large enough to preclude the random aggregation of votes, is substituted into equation (9) and, using the experimentally determined value of f_e, a value of m_{opt}, the required number of sampled sets of points, is determined. Thus the value of m_{opt} is data dependent. The expectation value, η_{opt}, is arbitrary and can be chosen to suit the needs of the application. Throughout the case study detailed at the end of this chapter, the value of η_{opt} was chosen to be 10.

7.2.7 Removal of Features from the Image

Once a shape has been successfully parametrized, it is necessary to remove it from the image. In the case of 'good' data, all points lying near the boundary curve of the parametrized shape are removed. To do this, the curve used to remove the points will have a width which is determined by the standard deviation in the estimated parameters. In the case of excessively noisy data, all points internal to that boundary are also removed in order that small fragments of noisy data internal to the shape do not remain to cause interference. Thus feature point removal is data dependent. Examples of feature point removal have been shown in Fig. 7.8 and Fig. 7.10. For example in Fig.7.8, the only remaining points associated with the objects are those forming the quarter arc of circle in the bottom right of the image and labelled **B**. Feature point removal, although sometimes incomplete as shown in Fig. 7.10, did not cause any problems in the running of the algorithm.

Now that we have a clear picture of the various stages of the algorithm, let's see what happens when we apply it to the real image data.

7.3 A Case Study

The following is a case study illustrating the application of the technique to the concurrent detection of circles and ellipses using real image data. As we said before, the case study should evaluate the algorithm over a range of conditions and suggest the limits beyond which it will breakdown. We can do this by simulating conditions which might reasonably exist in an industrial environment, variable lighting, shadows, reflections from the objects and damaged or occluded objects.

7.3.1 Edge Intensity Threshold and Connectivity Detection

To determine the robustness of the algorithm with respect the detection of connectivity, we have thresholded the edge image at 60%, 50% and 45% of its intensity range. The method of determining horizontal connectivity detailed in the previous section was used over this range of thresholds. To exceed the 60% threshold caused some small clusters of noise points which wrongly signalled connectivity. To go below the 45% threshold gave too few connected points. Connectivity detection can be tuned to operate in these extreme conditions, but here it is intended only to give an idea of the range of lighting and noise conditions over which a single detection method will work.

7.3.2 Segmentation

The results of detecting connected points and the segmentation generated using those results is shown in the leftmost column of Fig. 7.17 . In order to illustrate the 'non-detection' of a shape, in this particular test, only the horizontal connectivity detection process was activated. In this case, the detection of the occluded shape 2 on the top down scan of the image meant that the algorithm could not focus on the remaining shape 5. This shape was detected on a second pass of the image from the bottom up, right to left. Shape 5 therefore has a segment whose location is fixed by the connected point on the horizontal line segment at the bottom of the shape.

7.3.3 Automatic Stopping Criterion

Fig. 7.17 shows the results of processing for 1,400 and 14,000 sampling trials in the centre and rightmost columns respectively. Each shape was processed 10 times for each given number of trials. The resulting detected ellipses are shown in mid-grey. The variability of the result can be judged by the width of the curves they generate when superimposed on the original binary image. A general decrease in the width of the curves, corresponding to a reduction in the variability of the result, is seen with an increase in the number of sampling trials. The results, however, are not uniform and depend on the quality of the data processed. For the process to run automatically and where there may be fluctuations concerning the input data, it is necessary that a reliable algorithm should be able to judge automatically the quality of the image data and the amount of confidence it may have in any results of processing. The algorithm should be able to decide for itself the ultimate success of the processing and the degree of confidence which may be established in it. It should also be able to deduce when it has failed completely and either take alternative steps or alert the operator.

The stopping criterion detailed in subsection 7.2.6 was implemented using a value

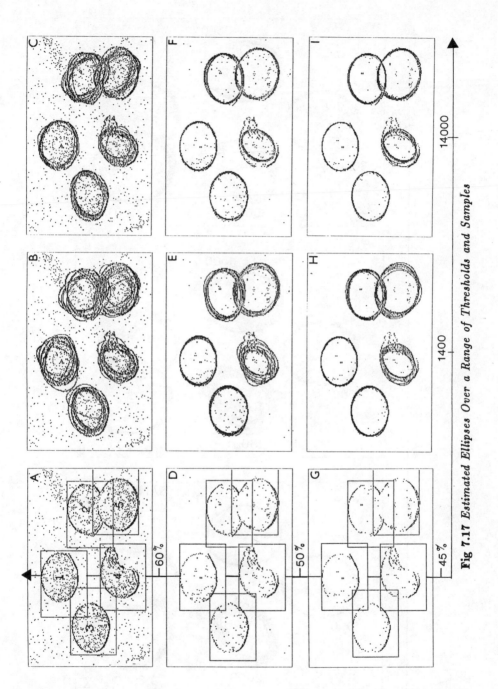

Fig 7.17 *Estimated Ellipses Over a Range of Thresholds and Samples*

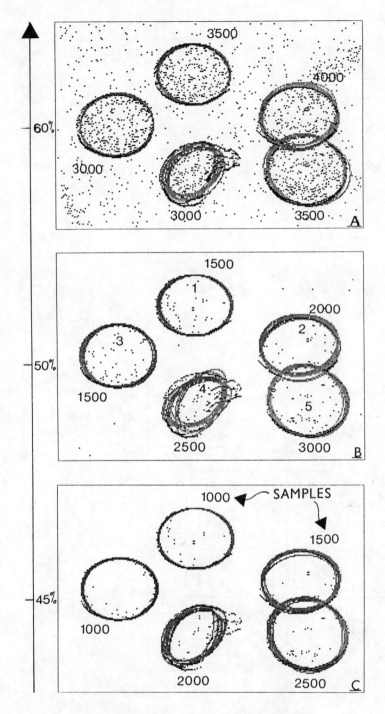

Fig 7.18 *Algorithm Working Automatically*

of 10 for η_{opt}. Fig. 7.18 shows the results of the algorithm running automatically. The number of sampling trials, m_{opt}, automatically determined for each object is shown next to the object. The segmentation is as shown in Fig. 7.17 . At the 60% threshold level the image data were 'cleaned up' by removal of single isolated noise points. This is a computationally trivial process and can be traded off against the increased accuracy and speed of the algorithm. The algorithm was run 10 times for each object and the resulting estimated ellipses superimposed on the binary edge image. In this way it is possible to see the variability of the results.

Comparing the results shown in Fig. 7.17 for the 65% threshold and those in Fig. 7.18 for the same threshold, it is clear that the removal of isolated noise points has quite remarkable results with respect to the accuracy of the estimated parameters. In particular, it should be noted that the estimated ellipses of Fig. 7.17 , image (C), where the estimates do begin to converge (shapes 1 and 3), the convergence is not strictly to the perceptual boundary of the object. This effect is caused by the many noise points internal to the boundary of the object and the uncertainty in the edge information to the left and right of the ellipse. The effect is greatly modified when the image is 'cleaned up', see Fig. 7.18 . The occluded objects (shapes 2 and 5) are detected with less certainty than the complete shapes and the algorithm automatically decides that it needs to take more samples when the data are degraded in this way.

7.3.4 Results

In order for the reader to make a quantitative comparison, the standard deviations for each set of 10 results are shown in the set of tables 1-5. Each table refers to a single object as labelled in Fig. 7.17 . Also shown in the tables are the number of feature points per segment and the automatically determined number of sampling trials, m_{opt}. The dependence of the standard deviation in the angle of rotation on the eccentricity of the ellipse precludes it from use as an estimator of the quality of the input data, accordingly it is not dealt with further. The isolated shapes, 1 and 3, show estimates with standard deviations ≤ 1 in all cases. Shapes 2 and 5, which are occluded, have some estimates with standard deviations ≥ 1 with relatively large numbers of sampling trials. This information will alert the algorithm to the poorer quality of the data. Shape 4, the 'chewed chocolate', is detected as an ellipse with a smaller eccentricity than that of the other shapes. This is sufficient to signal the dissimilarity of shape 4 to the other objects and also to locate and remove it from the field of view.

7.3.5 Coping with the Unexpected

Everything is fine if the algorithm were to handle only 'expected' data but it's also very important to know what happens if the 'unexpected' happens. How does the algorithm cope? Can it determine when something is going wrong? Fig. 7.19 shows an image composed of one 'expected' object and four 'unexpected' objects. The unexpected objects are two chocolates of a different type, one very damaged chocolate and some small pieces of chocolate. The edge image is shown in Fig. 7.20 .

This was thresholded at 60% of the range and the isolated noise points removed. The resulting binary image is shown in Fig. 7.21 . The objects are labelled 1 to 4.

Threshold	m_{opt}	Points	σa	σb	$\sigma \theta$	σx	σy
60%	3500	220	0.0	0.0	50.4	0.5	0.5
50%	1500	185	0.6	0.0	80.4	0.6	0.0
45%	1000	134	0.3	0.0	80.3	0.4	0.0

Table. 1 Results for Shape 1.

Threshold	m_{opt}	Points	σa	σb	$\sigma \theta$	σx	σy
60%	4000	254	0.4	0.7	68.2	0.5	1.3
50%	2000	206	0.7	1.0	50.7	0.4	1.3
45%	1500	141	0.8	0.9	51.8	0.5	0.9

Table. 2 Results for Shape 2.

Threshold	m_{opt}	Points	σa	σb	$\sigma \theta$	σx	σy
60%	3000	240	0.0	0.5	1.8	0.0	0.5
50%	1500	224	1.0	0.3	51.5	0.6	0.5
45%	1000	157	0.4	0.5	52.9	0.5	0.0

Table. 3 Results for Shape 3.

164

Threshold	m_{opt}	Points	σa	σb	$\sigma \theta$	σx	σy
60%	3000	306	0.6	1.6	18.8	1.2	0.5
50%	2500	269	1.5	0.8	13.7	2.6	0.5
45%	2000	199	1.8	1.3	12.0	0.9	0.5

Table. 4 Results for Shape 4.

Threshold	m_{opt}	Points	σa	σb	$\sigma \theta$	σx	σy
60%	3500	375	1.2	0.0	4.7	0.5	0.4
50%	3000	307	0.6	0.0	8.6	0.8	0.5
45%	2500	223	0.6	0.5	16.1	0.8	0.5

Table. 5 Results for Shape 5.

The algorithm was run automatically, 10 times for each object and the results are shown in Fig. 7.22 as superimposed mid-grey ellipses.

A table of the standard deviations for each run of 10 is shown in Table 6. Also shown are the number of sampling trials, m_{opt}, automatically deduced for each object. The expected object, shape number 1, is detected without any problems and the standard deviations of the parameters are in the range [0.3, 0.6] and the number of sampling trials is low, 1,500. Similarly object 2 causes no problems. It is detected as an ellipse of dimensions not associated with the object under detection. The information is sufficient to locate and remove the object. Object 3 is detected with a great deal of uncertainty with standard deviations in the range [0.3, 3.0] and a larger number of sampling trials, 3,000. This is because the silhouette of the object is not elliptical. It should, however, be possible from the information to locate and remove the object. Shape 4 is detected with standard deviations in the parameters in the range [0.7, 3.5] and a relatively large number of sampling trials. However poor the results might be with respect to inspection of the object, they still provide sufficient information for

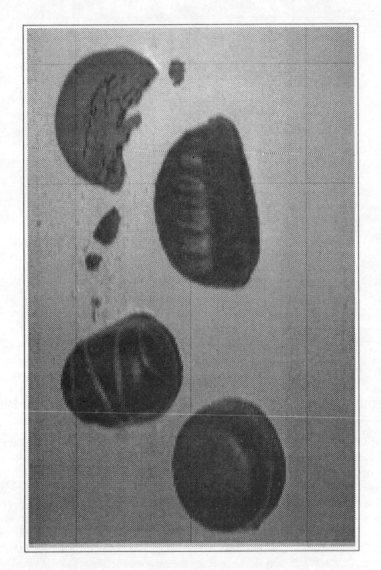

Fig 7.19 Real image of Mixed Chocolate Shapes

Fig 7.20 *Edge Image of Mixed Chocolate Shapes*

167

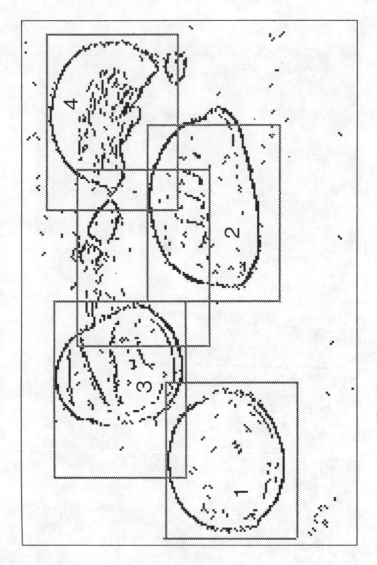

Fig 7.21 *Thresholded Image Showing Segmentation*

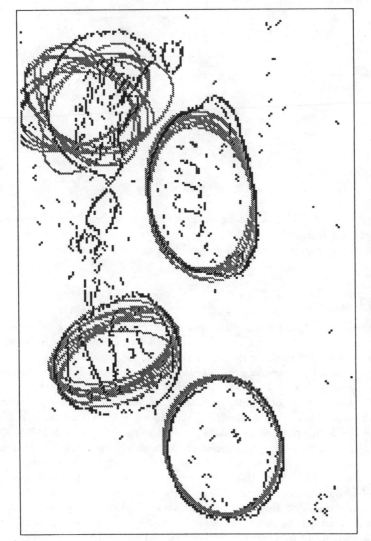

Fig 7.22 Detected Mixed Chocolate Shapes

Shape	m_{opt}	σa	σb	σx	σy
1	1500	0.3	0.5	0.6	0.3
2	2000	0.6	0.0	2.0	0.5
3	3000	0.3	3.0	2.0	0.6
4	3500	1.4	0.7	1.6	3.5

Table. 6 Results for Mixed Shapes.

the object to be identified as not belonging to the set of under detection and for it to be located and removed by a robot. The small pieces of chocolate are detected and can be either disregarded as being insignificant or the information used to alert the operator.

7.4 Discussion

Because Computer Vision recognition tasks are necessarily hierarchical processes, any implementation of the Hough Transform cannot be considered in isolation. Many previous attempts to improve its performance have depended on sophisticated pre-processing in order to determine the edge direction associated with each feature point. Two main approaches to edge detection exist; these are template matching and differential gradient operators. Both approaches estimate local intensity gradients with the aid of suitable convolution masks. In the case of template matching, it is usual to employ up to twelve convolution masks [Prewitt et al 1970], [Kirsch 1971], [Robinson 1977], [Abdou et al 1979]. A differential gradient operator needs only two masks but these may be required to operate over a large neighbourhood. For example, a properly implemented Marr-Hildreth operator requires convolution masks covering a 35 × 35 neighbourhood [Brady 1982]. It is clear that the computational burden is merely being shifted from the transformation to the preprocessing stage. This may not be a realistic option for industrial systems where any implementation of the technique should not only perform at least as well as the SHT but also run in a time commensurate with the needs of the application. In contrast, the DGHT requires only the simplest of edge detection procedures, the application of a five point Laplacian operator and a threshold. Moreover, it has been shown to work over a large range of thresholds.

The current trend in vision research is to recognize and use combinations of evidence extracted from the image data. The eye is not a one shot operator; it roams about

170

the field of vision stopping to focus on likely looking areas of interest. In this sense connectivity is a very powerful perceptive cue. A unique feature of the DGHT is that before the transformation is initiated, a search is made to locate a single connected feature point, (x_c, y_c). It may be thought expedient to obtain both edge and connectivity information in a single operation. For example, in edge maps obtained using the Canny edge detector [Canny 1986], all points are located on connected segments. However, the same objection exists to the large computational overheads induced by such preprocessing. For example, Lyvers et al [Lyvers et al 1988] have tested the Canny operator and found that it needed to be implemented using 180 masks and hence takes enormous computation time. Such investigations indicate that these sophisticated operators are useful mainly for the principles they illustrate concerning edge detection. The situation would only change if cheap suitably fast task specific hardware became available.

In comparison, the DGHT successfully uses a connectivity detection process that is computationally trivial requiring only additions over a small neighbourhood. In addition, global processing is not required as the algorithm terminates this operation once a connected point is found. The DGHT may in fact wrongly infer connectivity but it has been shown that such a wrong hypothesis is detectable and the system can therefore become self correcting. In addition, the complexity of the processing is low enough to allow the system the occasional wrong guess.

Once a connected point is identified, it is fixed and used with sets of $(n-1)$ randomly sampled image points to solve for the n parameters under detection. In this case, connectivity produces quite far reaching effects. Firstly, it reduces the number of individual points it is necessary to sample at each iteration from n to $n-1$. Secondly, there is a reduction in the number of calculations needed to accumulate the same threshold value as might be obtained using the methods of Xu et al [Xu et al 1990] or Bergen et al [Bergen et al 1990]. Thirdly, performance is enhanced because the fixing of one connected image point restricts the range of parameters calculated to that area of the transform plane associated with all possible instances of the shape under detection on which the connected point may lie. This lessens the effect of correlated noise associated with multiple objects.

In order to further reduce the effects of correlated noise, the DGHT segments the image. Sample points are then selected from this segment. The effect of segmentation is to further reduce the range of parameters over which voting may occur.

For the probabilistic Houghs to work efficiently, robust stopping criteria are needed concerning the optimum number of samples. This is because of the combinatorially explosive number of possible sets of points. It is important to note that a stopping criterion which is a function of some predetermined accuracy parameter, as proposed by Bergen et al, may fail if the data become unexpectedly degraded in a way that prevents the required accuracy from ever being attained. This may happen, for example, when an object becomes occluded or lighting conditions change for some reason not anticipated by the operator. The DGHT uses a stopping criterion that is a function of the quality of the image data expressed by the fraction of image points contributing to the shape under detection. A large contribution indicates good quality data and a high degree of confidence in the results.

Although the DGHT algorithm can be potentially applied to any analytically defined shape, each shape must be considered as a separate case. Segmentation is necessarily shape dependent and requires some knowledge of the dimensions of the shapes under detection. In addition, the choice of equation used to calculate the parameters is restricted to those which are both numerically stable and linear with respect to the parameters under detection.

If M is the total number of edge image points and T is the resolution in transform space, then for n parameters, an implementation of the SHT requires calculations on the order of MT^{n-1}. In comparison, the DGHT requires arithmetic operations on the order of n^3 for each set of n points [Press et al 1988]. However this can be reduced to n^2 if the matrix operations involved are distributed among n parallel processors. If there are i shapes in the image, then each shape will have associated with it m_i sampled sets of points. For the calculation of the parameters associated with all shapes in the image, this will require arithmetic operations on the order of

$$\sum_{j=1}^{i} m_j . n^3$$

Hence using the DGHT, the computational load is significantly reduced and is independent of the accumulator quantisation, T.

It has been shown that the excessive memory requirements of the SHT, which remain either untackled or unresolved with respect to the other PHT's, can be reduced from T^n to nT when using the DGHT. A further advantage is that peak detection is one-dimensional and each accumulator may be searched in parallel.

It is further shown that the DGHT can cope with both occlusion and the effects of correlated noise. In addition, the method provides an efficient feedback mechanism linking the accumulated boundary point evidence and the contributing boundary point data. It achieves this goal automatically and thus has the capability of detecting its own failure.

7.5 Conclusions

It has been shown that the present approach offers a significant improvement to previous suggested implementations of the Hough Transform. It is computationally less intensive and extremely portable. This makes it an attractive option for smaller companies where there is a need to make cost effective decisions concerning hardware.

The proposed method is more efficient in memory utilization. The SHT requires T^n memory allocations in order to maintain a unified n-dimensional accumulator. The Dynamic Generalized Hough transform (DGHT) requires only nT memory allocations, each one-dimensional accumulator being independent of all other $(n-1)$ accumulators.

Using the DGHT, the parameters can be calculated and accumulated independently. Peak detection is one-dimensional and can also be accomplished independently. The method provides an efficient feedback mechanism linking the accumulated boundary point evidence and the contributing boundary point data. It achieves this goal with an intelligent monitoring of the transformation, re-directing the processing as appropriate to the shape under detection. Most importantly, for industrial applications, it has the capability of detecting its own failure.

Appendix 1

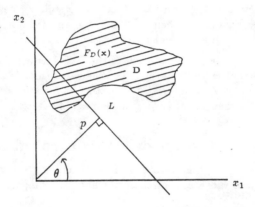

Fig 1.1 *Graphical representation of the Radon Transform.*

The Radon transformation of generalized functions concentrated on lines and curves are deduced using a geometric approach and a limiting process. It is shown that any curve may be replaced by its tangents for the purposes of transformation and that each tangent will produce a maximum value in transform space. Many aspects of the technique not immediately obvious in a purely analytical treatment become clear when expressed geometrically, and the need to evaluate complicated integrals is avoided.

1.1 The Radon Transform.

The Radon transform may be written in the convenient form suggested by Gel'fand et al, [Gel'fand et al 1966]

$$\Re\{F(\mathbf{x})\} = H(p,\xi) = \int\limits_{-\infty}^{\infty} d\mathbf{x}\, F(\mathbf{x})\delta(p - \xi\cdot\mathbf{x}) \tag{1}$$

In two dimensions the delta function, $\delta(p - \xi\cdot\mathbf{x})$, represents a line, L, of infinite length. ξ is a unit vector in the direction of the normal to that line and p is the algebraic length of the normal. It is of particular interest to consider the case in which the general function $F(\mathbf{x})$ is replaced by a particular function $F_D(\mathbf{x})$, where

$$F_D(\mathbf{x}) = \begin{cases} 1, & \text{in } D; \\ 0, & \text{otherwise.} \end{cases}$$

Fig. 1.2 illustrates the Radon transform of such a function. The shaded region represents the function $F_D(\mathbf{x})$. The line L acts as a probe or detector function and $F_D(\mathbf{x})$ as the object function. Whenever the line L and the domain D intersect the value of the integral is equal to the length of the intersection; otherwise it is zero.

The above definition leads quite naturally to the introduction of a shape descriptive element. The domain D may be taken to be a narrow band of uniform width whose shape is that of the curve of interest. A limiting process may then be applied to obtain a distribution concentrated along the curve of interest.

1.2 Generalized function concentrated on a line

Consider the case in which the domain D of the function $F_D(\mathbf{x})$ is an infinitely long vertical strip, $S(h)$, of width h, centred on the line $x_1 = x_{1_0}$; see Fig. 1.2 .

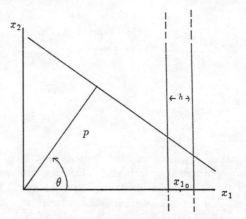

Fig 1.2 *Radon Transform*
of a thin vertical strip.

174

Then

$$F_{S(h)}(\mathbf{x}) = \begin{cases} 1, & |x_1 - x_{1_0}| \le \frac{1}{2}h; \\ 0, & \text{otherwise}, \end{cases} \tag{2}$$

and its Radon transform (here simply the length of the intersection of L with the strip) is given by

$$\Re\{F_{S(h)}(\mathbf{x})\} = \frac{h}{|\sin\theta|}. \tag{3}$$

Now let us introduce a weighting factor of $1/h$ and consider the function

$$F_h(\mathbf{x}) = F_{S(h)}(\mathbf{x})/h, \tag{4}$$

which has everywhere unit density per unit length along the strip, whatever the value of h. Then from the above result we have

$$\Re\{F_h(\mathbf{x})\} = \frac{1}{|\sin\theta|}. \tag{5}$$

Since this expression is independent of h it remains valid in the limit as $h \to 0$, the case of the unit-density δ-function distribution along the line $x_1 = x_{1_0}$. Thus we have shown that

$$\Re\{\delta(x_1 - x_{1_0})\} = \frac{1}{|\sin\theta|}. \tag{6}$$

Deans, [Deans 1981], arrives at the same result, basing his analysis on the work of Gel'fand et al, [Gel'fand et al 1966]. It is simple to show using the properties of shifting and linear transformation, that the corresponding result for a line whose normal subtends an angle ψ with the x_1 axis is

$$\Re\{\delta(p_1 - x_1 \cos\psi - x_2 \sin\psi)\} = \frac{1}{|\sin(\theta - \psi)|} \tag{7}$$

We note that the standardization of the equation of an arbitrary line to the form

$$p_1 = x_1 \cos\psi + x_2 \sin\psi \tag{8}$$

ensures that the corresponding δ-function distribution has unit linear density and is necessary for the validity of the result.

1.3 The general case

The result obtained in the previous section can be used to deduce the Radon transform of any unit density δ-function distribution lying along any smooth curve C. It is convenient to denote this function by $\delta(C)$. The only contribution to the integral defining the transform comes from the points of intersection of C with the scanning line L, and for the purposes of computation the curve can be replaced by its tangent in the neighbourhood of such points. Let us suppose that for given values of

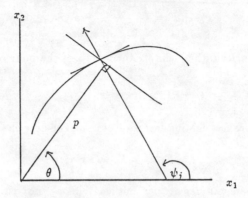

Fig 1.3 *Contribution to the Radon Transform*
of an arbitrary point on a curve.

p and θ there are n points of intersection, at which the normals to C make angles ψ_j $(j = 1, .., n)$ with the x_1 axis; see Fig. 1.3 . Then according to equation 7 we have

$$\Re\{\delta\,(C)\} = \sum_{j=1}^{n} \frac{1}{|\sin(\theta - \psi_j)|} \tag{9}$$

From this result it is clear that the essence of the problem is the determination of the points of intersection and the associated angles ψ_j.

Now let us suppose that the curve C is defined by an equation $f(\mathbf{x}) = 0$. In order to fulfil the unit-density condition we need to consider the transform not of $\delta\{f(\mathbf{x})\}$ but of $\delta\{w(\mathbf{x})f(\mathbf{x})\}$ where

$$w(\mathbf{x}) = \frac{1}{|\mathrm{grad}f(\mathbf{x})|} \tag{10}$$

is a weighting function defined on C. Explicit determination of $w(\mathbf{x})$ is unnecessary in practice, however, since the unit-density property is automatically realized by expressing the equations for the tangents in the normalized form of equation 7. For completeness we rewrite the result, equation 11, in terms of $f(\mathbf{x})$ giving

$$\Re\{\delta\,(w(\mathbf{x})f(\mathbf{x}))\} = \sum_{j=1}^{n} \frac{1}{|\sin(\theta - \psi_j)|} \tag{11}$$

From the fundamental result, (9) (equivalently (11)), it is evident that the Radon transform of any tangent to the curve is singular at $\theta = \psi_j$. Such singular points may be detected using a one dimensional convolution filter, see [Leavers et al 1987b].

To illustrate, the binary image of a parabola is shown in Fig. 1.4 . An intensity map of the transform plane of Fig. 1.4 is shown in Fig. 1.5 ; whilst the singular points detected in Fig. 1.5 after the application of a one dimensional filter are shown in Fig. 1.6 . From our knowledge of the location of these points we are able to reconstruct

176

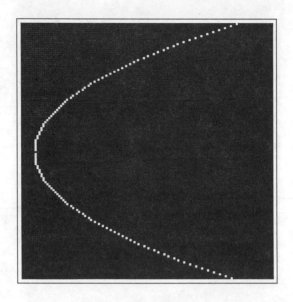

Fig 1.4 *Binary Image of a Parabola.*

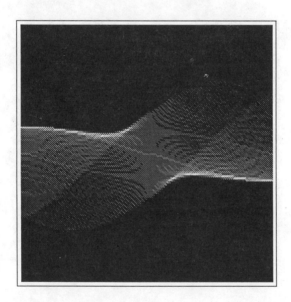

Fig 1.5 *Transform of Parabola.*

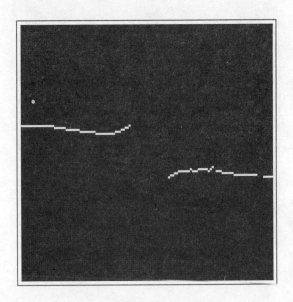

Fig 1.6 *Singular Points Detected.*

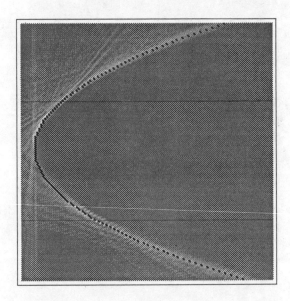

Fig 1.7 *Reconstruction of the curve*

the curve C as the envelope of the tangents. Fig. 1.7 illustrates this process. Each value of p and θ located in the transform plane by the convolution filter can be used to deduce the equation of a tangent to the curve in image space. In the reconstruction the points of intersection of the tangents will be most dense in the neighbourhood of the curve (shown in black) and hence maximum intensities are observed in this region.

1.4 Application to an ellipse

As an illustration of the method described above we consider the case of an ellipse, E, defined by the equation

$$\frac{(x_1)^2}{a^2} + \frac{(x_2)^2}{b^2} = 1 \tag{12},$$

The probe line of equation 1 may be written as:

$$p = \xi \cdot \mathbf{x} = x_1 \cos\theta + x_2 \sin\theta \tag{13}$$

An arbitrary point, P_ϕ, on E may be expressed as:

$$(x_1, x_2) = (a\cos\phi, b\sin\phi) \tag{14}$$

where ϕ is the parametric angle. In order to determine the values of ϕ corresponding to points at which L intersects E we substitute from equation (14) into equation (13) to obtain

$$p = a\cos\theta\cos\phi + b\sin\theta\sin\phi \tag{15}$$

This expression may be rewritten in the form

$$p = M\cos(\phi - \chi) \tag{16}$$

where

$$\left\{ \begin{array}{c} \cos\chi = \dfrac{a\cos\theta}{M} \quad, \quad \sin\chi = \dfrac{b\sin\theta}{M} \\[3mm] M = (a^2\cos^2\theta + b^2\sin^2\theta)^{\frac{1}{2}} \end{array} \right\} \tag{17}$$

Hence the required values of ϕ are

$$\phi_1, \phi_2 = \chi \pm \cos^{-1}\left(\frac{p}{M}\right) \tag{18}$$

provided that $|p| \leq M$. (If $|p| > M$ no intersection occurs.)

Now the equation of the tangent to the ellipse at P_ϕ is given by

$$\frac{x_1}{a}\cos\phi + \frac{x_2}{b}\sin\phi = 1 \tag{19}$$

which on reduction to the normalized form of equation 7 becomes

$$p_1 = x_1 \cos\psi + x_2 \sin\psi \tag{20}$$

179

where

$$\left\{ \begin{array}{c} p_1 = \dfrac{1}{K}, \quad \cos\psi = \dfrac{\cos\phi}{aK}, \quad \sin\psi = \dfrac{\sin\phi}{aK} \\[3mm] K = \left(\dfrac{\cos^2\phi}{a^2} + \dfrac{\sin^2\phi}{b^2} \right)^{\frac{1}{2}} \end{array} \right\} \qquad (21)$$

With ψ_1, ψ_2 defined by setting $\phi = \phi_1, \phi_2$ respectively in equation 21 we now obtain, using equation 11, the desired Radon transform

$$\Re\{\delta(E)\} = \left\{ \begin{array}{ll} \displaystyle\sum_{j=1}^{n} \dfrac{1}{|\sin(\theta - \psi_j)|}, & \text{when } |p| \leq M; \\[4mm] 0, & \text{otherwise.} \end{array} \right. \qquad (22)$$

With the aid of equations 17,18 and 21 it is readily shown that

$$\frac{1}{|\sin(\theta - \psi_j)|} = \frac{abK}{(M^2 - p^2)^{\frac{1}{2}}} \qquad (23)$$

180

Appendix 2

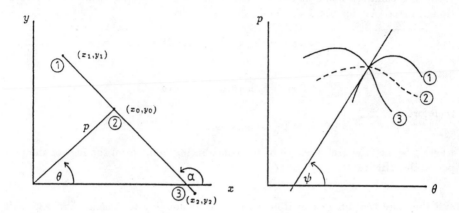

Fig 2.8 *Graphical representation of Hough transform.*

The Hough transform converts from point co-ordinates to line co-ordinates using the parametric representation:

$$r = x \cos \theta + y \sin \theta$$

For given x and y, which satisfy the above,

$$\frac{\partial r}{\partial \theta} = -x \sin \theta + y \cos \theta$$

$$= \tan \psi$$

Consider a straight line segment, l, having endpoints (x_1, y_1) and (x_2, y_2) i.e:

$$x = x_0 + p \cos \alpha$$
$$y = y_0 + p \sin \alpha$$

where:

$$\tan \alpha = \left(\frac{y_2 - y_1}{x_2 - x_1} \right)$$

and:

$$p = \pm((x - x_0)^2 + (y - y_0)^2)^{1/2},$$

(x_0, y_0) being the foot of the perpendicular from the origin to l. Now

$$\theta = \alpha - \frac{\pi}{2},$$

i.e:

$$\cos \alpha = -\sin \theta : \sin \alpha = \cos \theta$$

yields the common point of intersection of the corresponding family of curves in Hough space. At this point

$$\tan \psi = (-x_0 \sin \theta + y_0 \cos \theta) + p$$

but:

$$x_0 = r_0 \cos \theta, y_0 = r_0 \sin \theta$$

therefore:

$$\tan \psi = p$$

where p is the (algebraic) length of the contributing point from the foot of the perpendicular. Hence:

$$p_1 \leq \tan \psi \leq p_2$$

and therefore the maxima in Hough space corresponding to straight line segments occur as butterfly features and the angle subtended by the wings of the butterfly is determined by the positions of the end points.

For any straight line segment

$$-p_m \leq \tan \psi \leq p_m$$

where p_m is the maximum length permitted by the finite dimensions of the image. For a square image of side $2l$, $p_m = \sqrt{2}l$. For an $N \times N$ pixel image, having pixel dimension $(\Delta x)^2$, $l = \frac{N}{2}\Delta x$. In the corresponding $N \times N$ Hough image, having pixel dimension $\Delta r \Delta \theta$, the displayed slope, $\tan \chi$, is related to the true slope, $\tan \psi$, via

$$\tan \chi = \frac{\Delta \theta}{\Delta r} \tan \psi.$$

Hence the overall limits on the angles of the displayed wings are

$$-\sqrt{2}l \frac{\Delta \theta}{\Delta r} \leq \tan \chi \leq \sqrt{2}l \frac{\Delta \theta}{\Delta r}.$$

But $\Delta \theta = \frac{\pi}{N}$, and $\Delta r = \sqrt{2}\Delta x$ therefore:

$$-\frac{\pi}{2} \leq \tan \chi \leq \frac{\pi}{2}$$

i.e:

$$-58° \leq \chi \leq 58°$$

182

Appendix 3

For m points (x_i, y_i), where θ is an estimate of the angle the normal to the line makes with the positive x axis. The fitting process rotates the points so that the estimated line is horizontal. The rotation matrix is:

$$\begin{pmatrix} \sin\theta & -\cos\theta \\ \cos\theta & \sin\theta \end{pmatrix}$$

The least squares regression line:

$$y = mx + c$$
$$m = \tan\alpha$$

is calculated where:

$$m = \frac{\sum_{i=1}^{n}(\sin\theta(x_i - \bar{x}) - \cos\theta(y_i - \bar{y})(\cos\theta(x_i - \bar{x}) + \sin\theta(y_i - \bar{y}))}{\sum_{i=1}^{n}(\sin\theta(x_i - \bar{x}) - \cos\theta(y_i - \bar{y}))^2}$$

The fitted values of θ and r are given by:

$$\bar{\theta} = \theta + \alpha$$
$$\bar{r} = |(\bar{x}\cos\bar{\theta} + \bar{y}\sin\bar{\theta})|$$

Appendix 4.

This is an efficient method of calculating the Hough Transform using the normal parametrisation of the straight line. In its discrete form this is given by:

$$p_j = x_i \cos \theta_j + y_i \sin \theta_j$$

Let's consider exactly what we are asking the computer to do and the approximate amount of time this will take. We can do this by adding up the number of machine cycles it takes to complete each operation. The exact values vary from one machine to another, the following are fairly typical:

1. Go fetch values for $\sin \theta$ and $\cos \theta$ = 6

2. Two floating point multiplications   = 24

3. One floating point addition   = 3

4. One rounding operation and truncation operation   = 4

Total number of machine cycles = 37

This sequence is repeated j times for each image point. If $j=256$ and we have 2,000 image points this comes to 9,472 machine cycles just for the calculation of the p_j. If a machine cycle takes 1.0×10^{-6}s then it will take 18.95 seconds to complete the calculations.

In considering the optimisation of the calculation of the p_j one needs to rewrite the equation in a form which leads to a more computationally friendly form such as:

$$p_j = (x_i^2 + y_i^2)^{\frac{1}{2}} \cos \left(\theta_j - \tan^{-1} \left(\frac{y_i}{x_i} \right) \right)$$

which can be re-wrtten as:

$$p_j = A(x_i, y_i) \cos(\theta_j - \phi(x_i, y_i)) \tag{24}$$

This represents a cosine curve with an amplitude:

$$A(x_i, y_i) = (x_i^2 + y_i^2)^{\frac{1}{2}} \tag{25}$$

and a phase:

$$\phi(x_i, y_i) = \tan^{-1} \left(\frac{y_i}{x_i} \right) \tag{26}$$

Why on earth should equation (26) be more computationally friendly? Because it offers a way of substantially reducing the number of calculations necessary. Let's follow through why this should be.

184

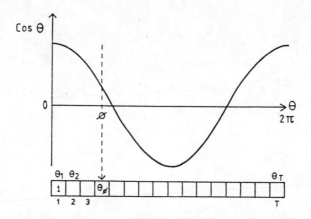

Fig 4.9 *Graphic representation of cosine look-up table*

It is clear from equation (25) and equation (26) that both the amplitude and the phase of the cosine curve are functions of x and y where (x, y) are simply the pixel co-ordinates. These are constant for a given value of i and may be pre-calculated, indexed by x and y, and stored in two, $2D$ arrays called look-up tables. This is possible because the range of values of the amplitude is small and it can be expressed as integer values without loss of accuracy to the result of the calculations.

Then we can have another look-up table whose elements are indexed by A_i and j. Each element in the array is the product of $A_i \cos \theta_j$. Fig. 4.9 shows elements of a single row of this two dimensional array. An integer value, ϕ_i, is obtained from the phase, $\phi(x_i, y_i)$ and is used as a pointer to the appropriate j index in this look-up table. Once we know this starting value we simply read-off j values in row A_i from the ϕ_ith element to the end of the row and then from the first element to the the $\phi_i - 1$ element. In this way we will obtain all of the p_j for that particular (x_i, y_i) using only one look-up and integer addition instruction per p_j. Let's work out a typical computation time, again for $j = 256$:

1. Two $2D$ look-ups, A_i, ϕ_i =   12

2. 256 $2D$ look-ups   = 1536

Total number of machine cycles = 1548

This is repeated 2,000 times for the whole image requiring a total of 3.1 seconds to complete all of the calculations.

Thus pre-calculating and storing the look-up tables can save considerably on the run time of the computation of the transformation. This requires a minimum of programming and no fancy hardware.

185

References

Abdou I.E. and Pratt W.K. *Quantitative Design and Evaluation of Enhancement and Thresholding Edge Detectors,* Proc. IEEE 67, pp 753-763, 1979.

Albanesi M.G. and Ferretti M. *Architectures for the Hough Transform: A survey,* Submitted to IEEE Trans. on Pattern Analysis and Machine Intelligence, December 1990.

Asada H. and Brady M.J. *The curvature primal sketch,* IEEE Trans. on Pattern Anal. and Mach. Intell., Vol. PAMI-8, No 1, January 1986.

Ballard D.H. *Generalizing the Hough Transform to detect arbitrary shapes. Pattern recognition,* 13, pp 111-122, 1981.

Ben-Tzvi D., Naqui A.A. and Sandler M.B. *Efficient parallel implementation of the Hough transform on a distributed memory system,* Image and Vision Computing, Vol. 7, No. 3, pp 167-172, 1989.

Ben-Tzvi D. and Sandler M.B. *Counter-based Hough Transform* Electronic Letters, Vol. 26, No. 11, May 1990.

Ben-Tzvi D. and Sandler M.B. *VLSI Implementation of the Hough Transform,* !EEE International Conference on Circuit and Systems, New Orleans, May 1990.

Bergen J.R., Shvaytser H., *A Probabilistic Algorithm for Computing Hough Transforms,* Journal of Algorithms, 12(4):639-656, December 1991.

Biedermann I. *Human image understanding: recent research and theory,* Computer Vision Graphics and Image Processing, Vol. 32, pp 29-73, 1985.

Blum H. *A transformation for extracting new descriptions of shape,* Symp. on models for the perception of speech and visual form, pp 362-380, MIT Press, 1967.

Bongiovanni G., Guerra C. and Levialdi S. *Computing the Hough Trtansform on a pyramid architecture,* Machine Vision and Applications, Vol. 3, No. 2, pp 117-123 1990.

Bracewell R.M. *The Fourier Transfrom and its applications*, McGraw Hill, 1965.

Brady M.J. *Smoothed Local Symmetries and local frame propagation*, Proc. IEEE Computer Science Conference on Pattern Recognition and Image Processing, 1982a.

Brady M.J. *Computational Approaches to Image Understanding*, Comput. Surveys, 14, pp 3-71, 1982b.

Brady M.J. *Representing Shape*, IEEE Int. Conf. on Robotics, 1984.

Brady M.J. and Asada H. *Smoothed Local Symmetries and their implementations*, MIT Artificial Intelligence Lab. Memo 757, Febuary 1984.

Brown C.M., Curtiss M.B. and Sher D.B., *Advanced Hough Transform implementations*, Proc. 8th IJCAI, pp 1081-1085, 1983.

Brown M.B. *Inherent bias and noise in the Hough Transform*, IEEE Trans. on Pattern Analysis and Machine Intelligence, Vol. PAMI-5, No. 5, September 1983.

Califano A., Bolle R.M. and Taylor R.W., *Generalized Neighbourhoods: A new Approach to Complex Parameter Feature Extraction*, Proc IEEE Conference on Computer Vision and Pattern Recognition, pp 192-199, 1989.

Canny J., *A Computational Approach to Edge Detection*, IEEE Trans PAMI 8, pp 679-698, 1986.

Casasent D.L. and Chatham R.L. *Hierarchical Fisher and moment based pattern recognition*, SPIE 504, 1984.

Casasent D.L. and Krishnapuram R. *Curved object location by Hough transformations and inversions*, PR, Vol. 20, 1987.

Davidson P.E. and Kruse B. *Distance checking algorithms*, Computer Graphics and Image Processing 11, 1979.

Davies E.R. *Circularity - a new principle underlying the design of accurate edge orientation operators*, Image and Vision Computing 2(3), 1984.

Davies E.R. *Design of cost-effective systems for the inspection of certain food products during manufacture*, Proc. 4th Conf. on Robotic Vision and Sensory Controls, London, Oct 1984.

Davies E.R. *PPL Manual*, National Physical Laboratories, Teddington Middx. England 1985.

Davies E.R. *Machine Vision*, Academic Press Limited, London, 1990.

Davis L. *Understanding shape - 1, angles and sides*, IEEE Trans. on Computers, C-26, pp 236-242, 1977.

Davis L.S. and Yam S. *A generalized Hough-like transformation for shape recognition*, University of Texas Computer Sciences, TR-134 1980.

Davis L.S. *Hierarchical generalized Hough transforms and line segment based generalized Hough transforms*, Pattern Recognition, Vol. 15, 1982.

Davis R.H. and Lyall J. *Recognition of handwritten characters - a review*, Image and Vision Computing, Vol. 4, pp 208-218, November 1986.

Deans S.R. *Hough transform from the Radon transform*, IEEE Trans. Pattern Analysis and Machine Intelligence. PAMI-3(2), March 1981.

Deans S.R. *Applications of the Radon transform*, Wiley Interscience Publications, New York, 1983.

Dirac P.A.M. *The principles of Quantum Mechanics*, 3rd ed., Oxford University Press, 1947.

Duda R.O and Hart P.E. *Use of the Hough transform to detect lines and curves in pictures*, Comm ACM 15, pp 11-15, January 1972.

Duda R. and Hart P., *Pattern classification and scene analysis*, Wiley 1973.

Dudani S.A. and Luk A.L. *Locating straight line edge segments in outdoor scenes*, Pattern Recognition Vol.10, pp 145-157, 1978.

Fisher A.L. *Scan Line Processors for image computation*, Proc. 13th Ann. Int. Symposium on Computer Architecture, pp 338-345, June 1986.

Fisher R.A. *The Maximum Likelihood Method*, Messenger Math. Vol. 41, pp 155-160, 1912.

Fischler M.A. and Firschein O. *Parallel Guessing; A Strategy for High-Speed Computation*, Pattern Recognition, Vol. 20, No. 2, p 297, 1987.

Forbes A.B. *Fitting an Ellipse to Data*, National Physical Laboratory Report, DITC 95/87 - December 1987.

Forman A.V *A modified Hough transform for detecting lines in digital imagery*, pp 151-160, SPIE, Vol. 635, Applications of Artificial Intelligence III, 1986.

Freeman H. *Computer processing of line drawings images*, Computing Surveys, pp 57-97, March 1974.

Freeman H. *Use of incremental curvature for describing and analysing two dimensional shape*, PROC PRIP, pp 437-444, Chicago 1979.

Fu K.S. *Syntactic pattern recognition and applications*, Prentice Hall 1982.

Gel'fand I.M., Graev M.I. and Vilenkin N.Ya. *Generalized functions* Vol. 5, Academic Press, New York, 1966.

Gerig G. *Linking image-space and accumulator-space. A new approach for object recognition*, Proc. of First Int. Conf. on Computer Vision, London, June 1987.

Gerig G. and Klein F. *Fast contour identification through efficient Hough transform and simplified interpretation strategies*, Proc. 8th Int. Conf. Pattern Recognition, Vol. 1, Paris, 1986.

Gonzalez C.R. and Wintz P. *Digital Image Processing*, Addison-Wesley, 1987.

Granland G.H. *Fourier preprocessing for hand printed character recognition*, IEEE Trans on computers, C-21, pp 195-201, 1972.

Grimson W. E. L. and Huttenlocher D.P. *On the Sensitivity of the Hough transform for Object Recognition*, IEEE Trans. on Patt. Analysis and Mach. Intell. Vol. 12 No. 3, p 255, 1990.

Hakalahti H., Harwood D. and Davis L.S. *Two dimensional object recognition by matching local properties of contour points*, Pattern Recognition Letters. Vol. 2, pp 227-234, 1984.

Hough P.V.C. *Method and means for Recognising complex patterns*, U.S. Patent No. 3069654, 1962.

Hu M. *Visual pattern recognition by moment invariants*, IRE Trans. on inform. theory, IT-8, pp 179-187, 1962.

Iannino A. and Shapiro S.D. *A survey of the Hough transform and its extension to curve detection,* IEEE Conf. on Pattern Recognition and Image Processing, New York 1978.

Ibrahim H., Render J. and Shaw D. *On the application of massively parallel SIMD tree machines to certain intermediate-level vision tasks,* Computer Vision Graphics and Image Processing, Vol. 36, pp 53-75, 1986.

Illingworth J. and Kittler J. *The adaptive Hough transform,* IEEE Trans on pattern analysis Vol. PAMI-9, no.5, 1987.

Illingworth J. and Kittler J. *A survey of the Hough transform,* Computer Vision Graphics and Image Processing 44, pp 87-116, 1988.

Illingworth J and Kittler J. *Measures of circularity for automatic inspection applications,* Proc. SPIE Int. Conf. on Automatic Inspection and Measurement, San Diego, SPIE 557.

Inigo R.M., McVey E.S., Berger B.J. and Wirtz M.J. *Machine Vision applied to vehicle guidance,* IEEE Trans Pattern Analysis and Machine Intelligence, Vol. PAMI-6, No.6, November 1984.

Jain A.N. and Krig D.B. *A robust Hough transform technique for machine vision,* Proc. Vision 86, Detroit, Michigan, 86.

Jolion J.M. and Rosenfeld A. *An O(log n) Pyramid Hough Transform,* Pattern Recognition Letters, Vol.9, p 343, 1989.

Jones D.S. *Generalized functions,* McGraw Hill, London 1966.

Kimme C., Ballard D.H. and Slansky J. *Finding circles by an array of accumulators,* Comm. of ACM. 18, 1975.

Kiryati N. and Bruckstein A.M. *Antialiasing the Hough Transform,* CVGIP: Graphical Models and Image Processing, Vol. 53, No. 3, May, pp 213-222, 1991a.

Kiryati N., Eldar Y. and Bruckstein A.M. *A Probabilistic Hough Transform,* Pattern Recognition, Vol. 24, No. 4, pp 303-316, 1991b.

Kirsch R. *Computer determination of the constituent structure of biological images,* Comput. Biomed. Res., Vol. 4, pp 315-328, 1971.

Krishnapuram R. and Casasent D. *Hough space transformations for discrimination and distortion estimation*, Computer Vision Graphics and Image processing 38, pp 299-316, 1987.

Kultanen P., Xu L. and Oja E. *Randomized Hough Transform (RHT)*, IEEE p 631, 1990.

Kultanen P., Xu L. and Oja E. *Curve Detection by an Extended Self-Organizing Map and the Related RHT Method*, Proc. INNC, 1990.

Kushnir M., Abe K. and Matsumoto K. *Recognition of handprinted Hebrew characters using features selected in the Hough transform space*, Pattern Recognition, Vol. 18, No. 2, pp 103-113, 1985.

Latto A., Mumford D. and Shah J. *The representation of shape*, IEEE Workshop on computer vision, Anapolis, 1984.

Leavers V.F. and Boyce J.F. *The Radon transform and its application to shape detection in computer vision*, Image and Vision Computing Vol.5, May 1987a.

Leavers V.F. and Miller G.F. *The Radon Transform of δ-function Curves*, Alvey Vision Club Conference, pp 335-340, Cambridge, September 1987b.

Leavers V.F. *Shape Parametrisation and Object Recognition in Machine Vision*, Doctoral Thesis, University of London, July, 1988a.

Leavers V.F. *Use of the Radon Transform as a Method of extracting symbolic representations of shape in two dimensions*, Unicom Symposium on Computer Vision and Image Processing, Proc. published by Kogan Page, London 1988b.

Leavers V.F. *Use of the Radon Transform as a Means of extracting Symbolic Representations of Shape in Two Dimensions*, Proc. of Alvey Vision Conference, pp 273-280, Manchester, 1988b.

Leavers V.F. and Sandler M.B. *An efficient Radon Transform*, 4th BPRA Meeting, Cambridge, 1988c.

Leavers V.F., Ben-Tzvi D. and Sandler M.B, *Dynamic Combinatorial Hough Transform for Straight Lines and Circles*, 5th Alvey Vision Conf., Reading, Sept 1989. Awarded Best Paper Prize for Contribution with Most Industrial Potential.

Leavers V.F. *The Dynamic Generalized Hough Transform*, First ECCV conf., Antibes, France, April 1990a.

Leavers V.F. *Active Intelligent Vision Using the Dynamic Generalized Hough Transform,* Proc British Machine Vision Conference, Oxford, September 1990b.

Leavers V.F., *The Dynamic Generalized Hough Transform,* SPIE Symposium on Electronic Imaging, Santa Clara, California, Febuary 1990c.

Leavers V.F. *It's probably a Hough: The Dynamic Generalized Hough Transform its relationship to the Probabilistic Hough Transforms and an application to the concurrent detection of circles and ellipses,* accepted for publication in CVGIP, March, 1992.

Li H., Lavin M.A. and LeMaster R.J. *Fast Hough Transform,* Proc. of 3rd workshop on computer vision, Bellair, Michgan, 1985.

Li H. *Fast Hough Transform for multidimensional signal processing,* IBM Research report, RC 11562, York Town Heights, 1985.

Lyvers E.R. and Mitchell O.R. *Precision Edge Contrast and Orientation Estimation,* IEEE Trans PAMI-10, pp 927-937, 1988.

Marr D. and Nishihara K. *Representation and recognition of the spatial organization of three dimensional shapes,* Proc. Royal Soc., B200, pp 269-294, London, 1978.

Marr D. *Computer Vision,* W. H. Freeman, 1980.

Mathematics Society of Japan *Encyclopaedic dictionary of mathematics,* Edited by Iyanaga S. and Y Kawada. MIT Press, London 1977.

Meer P., Baugher E.S. and Rosenfeld A. *The extraction of trend lines and extrema from multiscale curves,* Pattern Recognition, Vol. 21, No. 3, pp 217-226, 1988.

Merlin P.M. and D.J.Farber *A Parallel Mechanism for Detecting Curves in Pictures,* IEEE Trans. on Computers, Jan 1975.

Minsky M. *A framework for representing knowledge,* Psychology of vision, ed. P. Winston, McGraw-Hill, 1975.

Mostafari H. and Ollenburger R. *Image analysis using polarized Hough transform and edge enhancer,* SPIE Conf., Vol. 302, 1981.

Niblack W. and Petkovic D., *On Improving the Accuracy of the Hough Transform: Theory, Simulations and Experiments,* Proc. IEEE Conf. Computer Vision and Pattern Recognition, pp 574-579, June 1988.

Olson T.J., Bukys L. and Brown C.M. *Low level image analysis on an MIMD architecture,* Proc. 1st ICCV, pp 468-475, London, 1987.

O'Rourke J. *Dynamically quantised spaces for focusing the Hough transform,* 7th IJCAI, Vancouver, 1981.

O'Rourke J. and Sloan K.R. *Dynamic quantisation: two adaptive data structures for multidimensional spaces,* IEEE Trans PAMI-6, 1984.

Pavlidis T. *Waveform approximation through functional approximation,* IEEE Trans. on Computers, C-22, pp 689-697, 1973.

Pavlidis T. and Horowitz S. *Segmentation of plane curves,* IEEE Trans. on Computers, C-23, pp 860-870, 1974.

Pavlidis T. and Ali F. *Computer recognition of handwritten numerals using polygonal approximation,* IEEE Trans. on systems, man and cybernetics, SMC-5, pp 6101-6140, 1975.

Pavlidis T. and Ali A. *An hierarchical syntactic shape analyser,* IEEE Trans PAMI-2(9), 1979.

Petrou M. *On the Optimal Edge Detector,* Alvey Vision Conference, Manchester 1988.

Phillips E.G. *Functions of a complex variable with applications,* Interscience, London 1947.

Press W.H., Flannery B.P., Teukolsky S.A. and Vetterling W.T., *Numerical Recipes in C,* Cambridge University Press, 1988.

Prewitt J.M.S., *Object enhancement and Extraction,* In "Picture Processing and Psychopictorics", Academic Press, New York, 1970.

Princen J., Yuen H.K., Illingworth J. and Kittler J. *Properties of The Adaptive Hough Transform,* 6th Scandanavian Conference on Image Analysis, Oulu, Finland, June 1989a.

Princen J., Yuen H.K., Illingworth J. and Kittler J. *A Comparison of Hough Transform Methods,* Proc. IEE 3rd International Conference on Image processing and its Applications, University of Warwick, July 1989b.

Princen J., Illingworth J. and Kittler J. *Hypothesis Testing: A Framework for analysing and optimising the Hough Transform Performance,* Proc. 3rd Int. Conf. on Computer Vision, Osaka, Japan, 1990.

Radon J. *Uber die Bestimmung von Funktionen durch ihre Integralwerte langs gewisser Mannigfaltigkeiten. Berichte Sachsische Akademie der Wissenschaften Leipzig,* Math Phys Kl., 69, pp 262-267, 1917.

Ramer U. *An iterative process for polygonal approximation of plane curves,* CVGIP, Vol. 1, pp 244-256, 1972.

Risse T. *Hough Transform for the Line Recognition: Complexity of Evidence Accumulation and Cluster Detection,* Computer Vision Graphics and Image Processing, Vol.46, p 327, 1989.

Robinson G.S., *Edge Detection by Compass Gradient Masks,* Computer Graphics and Image Processing, Vol. 6, pp 492-501, 1977.

Rosenfeld A. and Johnston E. *Angle detection in digital curves,* IEEE Trans. on Computers, C-22, pp 874-878, 1973.

Rosenfeld A., Ornelas J., and Yubin Hung *Hough transform algorithms for mesh-connected SIMD parallel processors,* Computer Vision Graphics and Image Processing, 41, 1988.

Rosie A.M. *Information and Communication Theory,* Blackie, London, 1966.

Schwartz M. *Mathematics for the physical sciences,* Paris: Hermann, 1966.

Shapiro S.D. *Transformations for the computer detection of curves in noisy pictures,* Computer Graphics and Image Processing, Vol. 4, 1975.

Shapiro S.D. *Generalization of the Hough transform for curve detection in noisy digital images,* 4th Int. Joint Conference on Artificial Intelligence, Kyoto, 1978.

Shapiro S.D. *Feature space transforms for curve detection*, Pattern Recognition, Vol. 10, 1978.

Shapiro S.D. and Iannino A. *Geometric constructions for predicting Hough transform performance*, IEEE T-PAMI, Vol. 1, 1979.

Shaw A.C. *The formal picture description scheme as a basis for picture recognition*, Information and Control, 14, pp 9-52, 1969.

Silberberg T.M., Davis L. and Harwood D. *An iterative Hough procedure for three-dimensional object recognition*, Pattern Recognition, Vol. 17, No. 6, pp 621-629, 1984.

Sklansky J. *On the Hough technique for curve detection*, IEEE T-Comp, Vol. 27, 1978.

Sloan K.R. and Ballard D.H. *Experience with the generalized Hough transform*, 5th IJCPR, Miami Beach, 1980.

Sloan K.R. *Analysis of dot product space, shape descriptions*, IEEE T-PAMI, Vol. 4, 1982.

Smith E. and Medin D. *Categories and concepts*, Harvard University Press, 1981.

Stephens R.S., *Probabilistic Approach to the Hough Transform*, Image and Vision Computing Vol. 9. No. 1, Febuary 1991.

Stockman G.C. and Agrawala A.K. *Equivalence of Hough curve detection to template matching*, Comm ACM, Vol. 20, 1977.

Thissen F.L.A.M. *On equipment for automatic optical inspection of connecting lead patterns for integrated circuits*, Phillips Tech. Rev. 37, No.2, 1977.

Thomson R.C. and Sokolowska E. *Mineral Cleavage Analysis via the Hough Transform*, 4th Int. Conf. of BPRA, Cambridge, 1988.

Tsukune H. and Goto K. *Extracting elliptical figures from an edge vector field*, IEEE CVPR Conf., Washington, 1983.

Tsuji S. and Matsumoto F. *Detection of ellipses using modified Hough transformation*, IEEE T-COMP, Vol. 27, 1978.

196

Turin G.L. *An introduction to matched filters*, IRE Trans. Info. Theory, 6, 1960.

Van Veen T. M. and Groen F. C. A. *Discretization errors in the Hough Transform*, Pattern Recognition, Vol. 14, pp 137-145, 1981.

Wagner G. *Combining X-ray imaging and machine vision*, SME '87 Vision Conf. Detroit, June 1987.

Wallace R.S. *A modified Hough transform for lines*, IEEE conference on Computer Vision and Pattern Recognition, pp 665-667, San Francisco 1985.

Weschler H. and Sklansky J. *Automatic detection of ribs in chest radiographs*, Pattern Recognition, Vol. 9, 1977.

William H.P., Brian P.F., Saul A.T. and William T.V. *Numerical Recipes in 'C'*, Cambridge University Press, 1988.

Xu L., Oja E. and Kultanen P., *A New Curve Detection Method: Randomized Hough Transform (RHT)*, Pattern Recognition Letters, 11, pp 331-338, 1990.

Yam S. and Davis L.S. *Image registration using the Generalized Hough Transform*, IEEE PRIPS1, Dallas 1981.

Yuen H.K, Illingworth J and Kittler J., *Ellipse Detection Using the Hough Transform*, Alvey Vision Conference, Manchester, 1988.

Yuen S.Y.K. *Connective Hough Transform*, Proc. British Machine Vision Conference, Glasgow, 1991.

Zahn C.T. and Roskies R.Z. *Fourier Descriptors for Plane Closed Curves*, IEEE Trans on Computers, C-21, pp 195-201, 1972.

Index

Printing: Weihert-Druck GmbH, Darmstadt
Binding: Buchbinderei Schäffer, Grünstadt